The Prediction

The Pictorial Key to the Book of the Tarot

The Prediction Book of
THE TAROT

Madeline Montalban

JAVELIN BOOKS
POOLE · NEW YORK · SYDNEY

First published in the U.K. 1983 by Blandford Press,
Link House, West Street, Poole, Dorset, BH15 1LL.

Copyright © 1983 Triad
Reprinted 1984

This Javelin Books edition first published 1985 by
Javelin Books, Link House, West Street, Poole,
Dorset, BH15 1LL.

Reprinted 1986 (twice)

Distributed in the United States by
Sterling Publishing Co., Inc.,
2 Park Avenue, New York, N.Y. 10016.

Distributed in Australia by
Capricorn Link (Australia) Pty Ltd,
PO Box 665, Lane Cove, NSW 2066.

British Library Cataloguing in Publication Data
Montalban, Madeline
The prediction book of the Tarot
1. Tarot
I. Title
133.3'2424   BF1879.T2

ISBN 0 7317 1784 X

Typeset by Poole Typesetting (Wessex) Ltd.
Printed in Great Britain by The Guernsey Press Co. Ltd.

Contents

List of Illustrations

The Tarot cards shown in chapters 3 and 4 are from the following packs:

Minor Arcana
Aces – Rider/Waite
Twos – Aquarian
Threes – Conver/Marseilles
Fours – Royal Fez/Moroccan
Fives – Spanish
Sixes – Rider/Waite
Sevens – IJJ/Swiss
Eights – Aquarian
Nines – Oswald Wirth
Tens – Morgan Greer
Pages – Richard Gardner/Institute
Knights – Grimaud/Marseilles
Queens – Rider/Waite
Kings – Oswald Wirth

Major Arcana
0 The Fool – Rider/Waite
1 The Magician – Rider/Waite
2 The High Priestess – Royal Fez/Moroccan
3 The Empress – Richard Gardner/Institute
4 The Emperor – Morgan Greer
5 The High Priest – Royal Fez/Moroccan
6 The Lovers – Conver/Marseilles
7 The Chariot – Morgan Greer
8 Justice – Spanish
9 The Hermit – Morgan Greer
10 Wheel of Fortune – Oswald Wirth
11 Strength – Rider/Waite (With the number changed from 8 to 11)
12 The Hanged Man – IJJ/Swiss
13 Death – Spanish
14 Temperance – Grimaud/Marseilles
15 The Devil – Royal Fez/Moroccan
16 The Tower – Golden Dawn
17 The Star – Spanish
18 The Moon – Oswald Wirth
19 The Sun – Golden Dawn
20 Judgement – Douglas/Sheridan
21 The World – Grimaud/Marseilles

The cards on the cover are from the Grimaud/Marseilles pack.

Introduction

Reading the Tarot is not a simple operation. It needs more than a Tarot pack and a book of words telling you what the cards mean. It requires a great deal of memorising which cards link up with others, and a good lashing of that sixth sense which is pure clairvoyance. There are 78 cards in a full Tarot pack (22 Major Arcana or trump cards and four suits – Wands, Pentacles, Cups and Swords – each of which contains 14 cards). The number of permutations they can fall in is astronomical.

No book ever written tells you just what the different combinations can mean, for everything has to be referred to the peculiar circumstances and problems of the enquirer. Cards that would signify a business deal to some can mean an emotional entanglement for others. Those denoting a long journey for one person must obviously mean something else to a bed-ridden invalid.

Reading the Tarot is an art, which must be practised, cultivated and expanded each time it is done. Knowledge must be added to knowledge. You cannot begin too young, for if the power is born within you, you come early to the Tarot. And don't be afraid that you are too old, for mental power does not wear out.

What you must bear in mind if you want to read the Tarot is that it is not an easy method of divination; it requires more than merely memorising by rote the meanings of the cards, for one meaning can contradict another. You need the inner judgement that, I think, comes from love of the Tarot itself and enhances the sixth sense with which you were born. It needs imagination plus interpretation, and synthesis.

Acquiring a pack and book will not necessarily give you the power to read the cards, any more than buying a gas stove will make you an expert cook. But it is a beginning. The next step is to familiarise yourself with the cards. Let them 'talk' to you and reveal their special meanings for you. Practise on your friends. After a few tries you will either be sold on the Tarot for ever, or throw it away in disgust.

Remember, though, that divination tells you only what may happen if you don't do something about the situation described: it refers to possibilities not certainties. The true arcana of the Tarot teaches you just what you can do about it.

That is why, to my mind, its mysteries are far more useful than its divinatory aspect, but that, of course, is just a matter of opinion.

The Tarot, like any occult lore, can only be used and understood according to the powers that lie within you – in ratio to the ability of your own mind to penetrate and correlate its information. It can do no harm to the ignorant because, to them, it is unintelligible.

The more one studies the inner mysteries of the Tarot (apart from the fortune-telling symbolism, which is different) the more one realises that, properly understood, it is a book of wisdom in itself that reveals things to earnest students just when they are ready for the revelation. In delving into its hidden (and long lost) arcana, I have found that the complete meaning of the symbols of any particular card becomes suddenly apparent, perhaps long after I have stopped research on it.

In this respect, the study of the Tarot is very much like that of the Kabbalah, which hides what it wants to hide until it is ready to reveal it. Truly magical (or occult) systems do this. The words may be there, but their sense only becomes clear when you really need to understand it. That is how occult secrets are hidden; one's own ignorance acts as a blindfold which desire for enlightenment starts to loosen, though it doesn't fall away until you are ready to use the knowledge wisely.

Tarot cards just carry pictures. The main designs all agree, although some contain more detail than others: The power of the Tarot lies not in the cards themselves, but in the knowledge the reader possesses.

Each Tarot card is as many-sided as a faceted jewel. Not one book but many would be needed to describe the complete occult lore which lies behind each card, for they are keys, but in code, to a series of interlocking occult mysteries. What is more, there are planes of understanding of the Tarot, and to look on it merely as a pack of fancy cards intended just for fortune-telling is not to understand it at all.

The arcane, or 'mystery' side of the Tarot is not contained within the covers of any book, though fragments of it are scattered through thousands. But you might not recognise such fragments as Tarot lore unless you had an extensive knowledge of ancient religions and customs, and what is called the Law of Correspondences.

If it were possible to collect, interpret and write down all the mysteries concealed behind the symbol-graph called the Tarot, we would possess the Book of Thoth, or book of all wisdom.

The term 'Book of Thoth', therefore, does not refer to an actual book at all, but to the manifold, completed mysteries that lie behind each card, and which have been sought from time immemorial.

I have spent many years reconstructing some of these fragments of knowledge and still have only pieced together a fraction of the whole. And you are welcome to share my knowledge.

CHAPTER 1
Consulting the Tarot for Guidance

Many people believe that the Tarot is very complicated to read and learn – too much so for the answering of simple questions. This may be because expert interpreters of the Tarot often fail to make it clear that the exoteric and esoteric meanings of the cards can be separated.

There are hundreds of ways of setting out the Tarot but if you, like me, sometimes want to use it for answering specific questions in a certain way, then you need a mundane translation of the cards and a simple method of laying them out that does not need too much synchronisation. Most people consult the Tarot for four basic reasons: for questions concerning love, finance, their families and proposed (or feared) changes of conditions.

There is no reason at all why you should not be able to answer such questions quite simply for yourself and you should lay aside the fallacious belief that this is inadvisable. The only danger in interpreting the cards on your own behalf lies in the possibility of manipulating the lay-out's interpretation to give you the answer you want: so if you feel that you may be in danger of doing this, don't waste time trying to read the cards for yourself as it would obviously be pointless.

However, if you are convinced that you really want to know the answer to a question that is bothering you and are capable of being honest with yourself, I will explain simple methods of doing so. Firstly, before you begin your reading, concentrate on the question you want answered for a while (only ask one question of a spread or you will get a confusing response) and vow that you will interpret the cards as fairly to yourself as you would for anyone else for whom you were reading them: do not colour them with your own desires.

To answer a love question

Pick out the suit of Cups from the Tarot pack as this suit is used for all questions concering heart interests and corresponds to the Hearts suit in a pack of playing cards.

If you are a woman, the Queen of Cups represents yourself and the

King symbolises the man you love. If you are a male, simply reverse that order: the King stands for you. Shuffle the fourteen Cups cards well, then cut them into three heaps.

Without altering the order of the cards in each pile, look through each heap in turn until you find the one which contains the card representing yourself. When you have done this, set aside the other two heaps as these cards will not be needed. Next, taking the heap in which the card representing you lies, lay the cards out in a semi-circle, face upwards, in the order in which they fall.

Now, take the 22 Tarot trumps and discard all but the following cards: 0. The Fool, 1. The Magician, 3. The Empress, 6. The Lovers, 7. The Chariot, 9. The Hermit, 12. The Hanged Man, 13. Death, 14. Temperance, 15. The Devil, 16. The Tower, 18. The Moon, 19. The Sun, 21. The World.

Shuffle these 14 trumps, cut once, lay the bottom heap of the cut on the top heap, then deal out one trump on each of the Cup suit cards in your semi-circle. The trump that falls on the card which represents you contains the answer to your question and those which fall on the other cards in the spread signify how this will come about.

Obviously, it is not feasible for me to interpret all the possible permutations that could occur, so here are the meanings of each of the Cups suit and each of the Major Arcana cards used for this spread. You need, of course, only read those which actually fall in the lay-out.

King   A sympathetic man. *Reversed* You are counselled to be on your guard against this man's charm.

Queen   A charming woman. *Reversed* You will regret her influence over you.

Knight A lover, not the one you are thinking about. *Reversed* One who will not be straightforward with you.

Page   The bearer of a message. In some cases, a birth. *Reversed* Trickery.

Ten   The place in which the enquirer resides and the esteem of his friends. *Reversed* Friction in the family circle.

Nine   Success and your wish granted. *Reversed* The inquirer's success may be marred by his or her imprudence.

Eight   A happy marriage to one you least expect. *Reversed* Happiness, a proposal and much gaiety.

Seven   An unexpected stroke of good luck. *Reversed* Good fortune. Either way up this card denotes a successful romance.

Six   The shadows of the past will have a bearing on the future. *Reversed* This influence is yet to come.

Five   A marriage or happy and triumphal conclusion to a love affair, coupled with monetary gain. *Reversed* Unexpected news or visitor.

Four   Outside influences endanger your love affair. *Reversed* A new and pleasant friendship.

Three   Your hopes will be fulfilled. *Reversed* Danger of disgrace or an unfortunate accident.

Two   Reciprocated love, but danger from miserliness. *Reversed* Love is discouraged or rejected. Do not commit yourself.

Ace   A happy gathering. Good news and rejoicing. *Reversed* The beginning of a love affair.

0 *The Fool* Want of thought and heedless actions. *Reversed* Muddled thinking and self-induced problems.

1 *The Magician* A change of circumstances (self-induced and hastily decided in the case of a male querent). *Reversed* This change may prove unfortunate.

3 *The Empress* Fertility and domestic happiness. *Reversed* Disharmony and lack of the desired union.

6 *The Lovers* The loved one hesitates, not knowing his/her own feelings. *Reversed* Love problems, a broken romance and heartache.

7 *The Chariot* Triumph over mundane obstacles to the desired love affair. *Reversed* Discouragement and quarrels.

9 *The Hermit* Be cautious of subtle intrigues. *Reversed* Your own timidity stands in the way of romantic happiness.

12 *The Hanged Man* Upright or reversed, when lying on the card of the querent, this card overshadows all others and signifies that the querent's love affair is doomed to failure.

13 *Death* If falling on the querent's card, it means abandon all your romantic hopes as no good can come of them, no matter how propitious they may now seem.

14 *Temperance* A rich marriage or union with one who will become rich. *Reversed* Be discreet, watch you tongue.

15 *The Devil* A strong temptation that must be resisted or great sorrow will result.

16 *The Tower* Secrets could become public. *Reversed* Ruin and disgrace if you persist in your present course.

18 *The Moon* You are regarding your beloved through rose-tinted spectacles and are likely to be disillusioned.

19 *The Sun* This is a wholly beneficient card and modifies all threatened evil in any lay-out.

21 *The World* A happy omen of success in your hopes, health and fertility. *Reversed* These hopes may be delayed but not extinguished.

Although the mundane meanings of the whole Cups suit and the 14 trumps to be used have been given, you will not use all these for your final reading and can ignore those cards which do not fall in the spread. The cards which fall on the one representing the querent are of prime importance. If a woman, and the King falls anywhere in the spread (or the Queen in the case of a male querent), the trump lying on that card is of secondary importance. Third in importance are those trumps which fall on the ten, eight, seven or nine (this latter being the wish card).

Most lay-outs present no more than six suit cards and six trumps to be read. These are read in conjunction, pair by pair, using the interpretations listed. The meaning of the spread as a whole will emerge clearly once the querent's card and that of the loved one have been considered in relation to the other cards in the spread.

To answer a financial question

At one time or another everybody suffers from financial worry and feels that they cannot see their way ahead. At such times, the Tarot can offer useful guidance, but it cannot be too strongly emphasised that however bright the Tarot's forecasts may be, the cards must be read on the assumption that the querent is doing all in his/her own power to bring their promise to fruition.

Financial problems are relieved by the application of a backbone not a wishbone and, according to the effort you make to help yourself, so may you expect results. The Tarot is to guide your efforts, not to replace them. So, avoid hoping for miracles, like backing a winner or winning the pools, when you consult the Tarot. Such things do happen, but seldom when you feel you need them most.

The method used for selecting and laying out cards for a spread concerning a fincancial question is the same as that already described, except that the suit of Pentacles is used. In some Tarot packs this suit has a particularly symmetrical design and it can be difficult to distinguish which way up some of the numbered cards should be. So it is a good idea to check that yours are easy to distinguish and, if they are not, to put a small mark in one corner to indicate the top of the card for you will need to know whether it falls upright or reversed in the spread.

As with the previously mentioned spread, only certain of the Tarot trumps are used though, again, these are selected and laid on the suit cards in the manner already explained. Here, then, are the meanings for the cards in the Pentacles (sometimes called Deniers or Coins) suit and for the selected Major Arcana cards for a spread concerning financial prospects.

King   Represents the querent, if male. *Reversed.* A pressing creditor.

Queen   Represents the querent, if female. *Reversed* The main cause of the monetary difficulty.

Knight   A new acquaintance who will add to rather than resolve your problems. *Reversed* A quarrel and scandal.

Page   Good news. *Reversed* Bad news and financial loss.

Ten   A monetary gain. *Reversed* A small gain.

Nine   A new job or a substantial income which is the result of your own endeavours.

Eight   A peaceful, prosperous phase. *Reversed* Strife and disorder.

Seven   A monetary gain or gift. *Reversed* Financial worry which will not be relieved by borrowing, so best avoid it.

Six   Financial wrangles; possibly a lawsuit resulting in loss. *Reversed* Unexpected resources will become available, but there may be a hidden snag.

Five   An unhoped for sum of money. A windfall that will compensate for former losses. *Reversed* A slight financial gain.

Four   Socialising could lead to further problems: not a time for setting financial sprats to catch mackerels. *Reversed* Foolish extravagance.

Three   A business proposal or undertaking. *Reversed* It will not lead to any significant result.

Two   Your financial plight is serious and requires all your efforts. *Reversed* A sudden or unexpected happening which may be auspicious or otherwise according to the trump card read with this one.

Ace   A new project or enterprise that will entail financial gain; also gifts. *Reversed* A small gain or legacy.

Only the following Major Arcana cards are needed for this spread:

1 *The Magician* A change of financial position. *Reversed* An unfortunate one.

2 *High Priestess* A more serious outlook is needed; do not fritter away your energies on trivia. *Reversed* This warning is emphasised.

7 *The Chariot* Providence comes to your rescue in the nick of time. *Reversed* You may ignore opportunity's knock.

8 *Justice* You will get what you really deserve – either way. *Reversed* Do not go to law regarding your problem as the judgement will be adverse.

10 *The Wheel* If this card falls on that of the querent it signifies that whatever the past monetary position has been, this will be reversed. *Reversed* If allied to unfavourable cards, your ambitions will be delayed. Financial prospects are fading.

11 *Strength* Attainment of the desired end. Success is assured if this card falls on that of the querent or on a fortunate suit card. *Reversed* You are cautioned not to misuse your triumph.

15 *The Devil* You will have to face a temptation to solve your problem by unlawful means. *Reversed* The temptation may be too strong to resist.

16 *The Tower* Financial luck is on the wane so, if you are in serious difficulties, plan on making a fresh start. *Reversed* If lying on a fortunate suit card, especially the 7, it presages an unexpected legacy, gift or windfall.

19 *The Sun* A fortunate card signifying that providence will come to your aid in a most mysterious way.

21 *The World* Relief from your most pressing worries lies ahead. *Reversed* As when upright, but delayed.

As with the previous spread, the trump and suit cards are read in pairs and will give a clear indication of what lies ahead. For a financial query, the most important cards to consider are those that lie to either side of the querent's card, for these will give the main indications.

Finally, if the Tower (No. 16) falls on that of the querent, let him not despair because, evil-omened as this card is, I have found by long practice that, although it denotes what seems to be a disaster at the time, this often turns out to be the start of a new and better avenue of life in the long run.

To answer a family question

The suit of Wands (sometimes called Rods or Staves) is used for answering questions that concern your family and it must be borne in mind that when reading for family affairs, you are the interpreter not the querent. The method, therefore, differs slightly from that already given.

In seeking Tarot guidance on behalf of a family member, you must be detached and dispassionate and must avoid the pitfall of considering the repercussions on yourself, no matter how close a relative the querent may be. For the purposes of such a spread, the term family refers only to your father, mother, husband (or wife), brothers (or sons) and sisters (daughters). In-laws, aunts, uncles, nieces, nephews, etc. are designated friends, not family, in such a spread. So, using the Wands suit only, first identify the card which represents the querent (or the one for whom you are enquiring) from the following list:

Father or husband – King of Wands
Mother or wife – Queen of Wands
Brother or son – the Knight
Sister or daughter – the Page

The complete Wands suit is then shuffled, cut, selected and laid out in the usual manner, using only those cards in the heap containing the querent's card. But, when we come to the trump cards, the method is slightly different. Again, only certain trump cards are utilised in the spread, this time Nos. 3, 4, 7, 8, 9, 10, 12, 15, 17, 18, 19 and 22.

Shuffle these twelve cards well, cut once, from left to right. Now, place the left-hand heap on top of the right-hand pile before placing a trump card on every suit card in the semi-circle. If you have not enough trump cards to cover each suit card it does not matter and if you have any trump cards left over, simply set them aside.

The Major Arcana card which lies on top of the querent's card should be read first as this contains the heart of the matter. The cards lying to the right and left of the querent's card are next in importance. Again, it is the convention that the cards should be read in pairs.

King Represents father or husband, also successful business dealings. *Reversed* Danger.

Queen Represents mother or wife. *Reversed* Suspicion, jealousy and mistrust.

Knight Brother or son; also prudence in money matters. *Reversed* Ill luck due to carelessness over finance or the imprudence of a friend.

Page Sister or daughter; also well-regulated financial affairs. *Reversed* Extravagance or thriftlessness.

Ten An unfamiliar town; sometimes travel abroad. *Reversed* An undertaking is apt to go awry.

Nine Good judgement and complete honesty will solve the problem. *Reversed* Underhand dealings and disloyalty.

Eight If the querent is a male, this card denotes a dark-haired woman of upright character whom he may marry. *Reversed* Worry and deception due to a woman.

Seven Legacies, business gains, assured success of any question. *Reversed* Business affairs in a precarious state.

Six Complete or partial failure of a project. *Reversed* Abandon any hope of a successful outcome.

Five Triumph over . impediments. Sometimes, a successful love affair. *Reversed* Unhappy love.

Four Pleasure and social life. *Reversed* An unsympathetic atmosphere.

Three Wealth and renown are indicated if the trumps with this card are good. In any case, a stroke of luck is indicated. *Reversed* The laying of the foundations of a successful career.

Two Crossings in love, trouble, unforeseen business difficulties. *Reversed* A happy communication.

Ace The start of a new undertaking. *Reversed* There will be many difficulties to overcome; care and prudence will be needed.

3 *The Empress* Domestic happines. *Reversed* Disharmony.

4 *The Emperor* An influential man who can help or hinder the querent. *Reversed* One who will show pity and clemency.

7 *The Chariot* Victory over obstacles. *Reversed* Victory will be preceded by apparent, defeat and great discouragement, so perseverence is indicated.

8 *Justice* Help from an unexpected source. *Reversed* Warns against litigation and/or an adverse decision against the querent in the matters inquired into.

9 *The Hermit* Discretion in personal matters is needed. *Reversed* Gossip may cause you grief.

10 *The Wheel* Changes are imminent. *Reversed* They may not be to your liking.

12 *The Hanged Man* Circumstances will need careful handling. *Reversed* Sacrificing yourself for another will be of no avail.

15 *The Devil* Inter-family conflict. *Reversed* An outsider threatens to disrupt family unity.

17 *The Star* Despite appearances, all could turn out well. *Reversed* The matter is beyond help, so abandon worry and make new plans.

18 *The Moon* Self-deception and the deceit of others are indicated by this card however it falls.

19 *The Sun* A well-omened card indicating family happiness and/or the return of a wanderer.

22 *The Fool* Extravagance and impetuous action will bring regret unless curtailed. *Reversed* Health may be below par and thus impair the querent's judgement.

To decide whether or not a change will be for the better

When consulting the Tarot as to whether or not it is advisable to make changes in your romantic, business, financial or domestic affairs, you must first be completely honest with yourself before posing the question. Decide exactly what you hope to gain by making a change because confused or wishful thinking will only result in an unsatisfactory answer from the cards.

Also, take an occult hint and never contemplate making a change from any job, place or situation in which you have been happy. If you do, the change will prove unfavourable. But, if you are decided on a change and wish to consult the Tarot for guidance, first select the Minor Arcana suit which corresponds to your complexion from the following:

Wands – very fair-complexioned people.
Cups – mid to light brown hair and blue or grey eyes.
Pentacles – dark-haired people with blue, grey, hazel or green eyes.
Swords – very dark-complexioned people.

In each case, the querent's card is represented by the King (if male) or Queen (if female) of the appropriate suit.

The selected cards are shuffled in the usual manner, cut into three heaps and that which contains the card representing the querent is used. These cards are then laid out in order and those that lie immediately to the left and right of the significator (the card representing the querent) are those of prime importance: the one to the right represents what will be accomplished by your efforts and the one to the left indicates the influences of fate.

As usual, only selected cards from the Minor Arcana are used; these are laid on the suit cards in the normal manner and the cards read as pairs. Thus, armed with foreknowledge, you will be able to exercise your free will, either going ahead with the proposed change or abandoning the project. The choice is yours to make.

King The querent, if male; or the man closest to the female querent.

Queen The querent, if female; or the woman nearest the male querent's heart.

Knight A new friend of the opposite sex. *Reversed* A helpful friend.

Page A new friend of the same sex.

Ten A fateful change; for the good if upright and vice versa if reversed.

Nine A fruitful change; well-starred. *Reversed* Some time will elapse before you make it.

Eight The hand of fate in your affairs.

Seven Impending events for good or ill depending on the Tarot trump which covers this card.

Six A new romance. *Reversed* It will not prove satisfactory.

Five Unsettled conditions; for some people this denotes travel. *Reversed* The outcome will be good in the (very) long run.

Four Domestic disharmony results from change. *Reversed* A removal from the home.

Three Personal struggles against difficulties. *Reversed* These will be difficult to overcome.

Two Contentment. *Reversed* Danger of accepting too little from life.

Ace This signifies the Sword of Fate that cuts all knots. *Reversed* Destiny takes a hand; matters are not under your control.

0 *The Fool* You will be the originator of your own troubles, so do not make any rash decisions.

1 *The Magician* Occult guidance or intuition.

2 *The High Priestess* Someone who has already received guidance. *Reversed* Not a good omen.

6 *The Lovers* A love affair which will prove unfortunate if this card falls reversed.

7 *The Chariot* A very good omen; any change being contemplated should prove favourable.

8 *Justice* You will be judged and rewarded according to your merit.

9 *The Hermit* An isolated position, perhaps loneliness. *Reversed* Great responsibilities that you will have to shoulder alone.

11 *Strength* Triumph over present conditions. *Reversed* Unfortunate influences will delay the achievement of your aims, but such obstacles can be overcome.

12 *The Hanged Man* The change you propose making will not be advantageous. *Reversed* This proposal will cause long-lasting problems.

13 *Death* This signifies the death of hopes, so do not tempt fate. *Reversed* Personal problems, perhaps illness.

15 *The Devil* Only the very adventurous and entirely fearless should follow any course marked by this card. *Reversed* Strong and malign temptation which will be very hard to resist.

16 *The Tower* Complete holocaust in your private life, often followed by an entirely new direction. This is a very fateful card. *Reversed* The interpretation is modified.

19 *The Sun* A fortunate omen. Go ahead with your plans if this card lies on the card to the left or right of the significator as, in these positions, this card overrules all others unless No. 16 (the Tower) falls on that of the querent. If the latter is the case, the Sun signifies that

the new beginning, built on the ruins of the old, will lead to a brighter life than you have ever known.

21 *The World* A very happy omen of good fortune ahead. *Reversed* This will come through your own efforts.

CHAPTER 2
Consulting the Tarot for Divination

The Tarot cannot be learned easily, and one never stops learning about it, but nobody will claim to be master of it unless they are foolish for it is the book of wisdom and initiation, the Book of Thoth, the recorder-teacher, god of the ancient Egyptians.

The Tarot never lies, but it is certainly one of the most difficult forms of fortune-telling. So much depends upon the knowledge of the Tarot reader and on how he or she responds to the inspiration the cards give. It has to be translated according to the nature and problems of the querent.

Though I know that certain so-called Tarot readers sometimes give readings from the Major Arcana alone, this is, in fact, not at all reliable because the Major Arcana represents the causes, while the Minor – containing the suits of Cups, Wands, Pentacles and Swords – influences the effects. Every effect has a cause.

A reliable reading is best obtained by the enquirer shuffling the Major Arcana cards, then cutting these into three, placing the first heap on the second, and the third on top of that. Next the cards are turned face up, dealt out as they come from one to 12, in two lines of six.

Next, do the same with the Minor Arcana, first letting the enquirer shuffle the cards, cut into three, placing the first heap on top of the second, and the third on top of that. The cards are then turned picture side up and dealt as they come, on top of the Major Arcana cards, from one to 12 in two lines of six.

As an example, if position 11, the Star (No. 17 in the Major Arcana), has the ill-omened Nine of Swords in the Minor Arcana on top of it, how would you translate this?

First of all, remember that the Major Arcana cards are always more important because they carry more weight than those of the Minor Arcana. So, in the above situation the enquirer's hopes seem to offer little promise, rather the reverse, as there are many obstacles to be overcome (the Nine of Swords). But the enquirer will put up a good fight. This outcome is indicated by the Swords which always represent strife in some form. Eventually, the enquirer's hope will be realised because the Star, card No. 17, overrides the Nine of Swords.

The Major Arcana cards always override those of the Minor. Equally, if the enquirer had the fortunate Nine of Cups in the first place, but this lay on top of No. 16, the Tower – a Major Arcana card – the enquirer could obtain his wish, although this may be followed by disaster and ruin. So, in this example it would be better if the enquirer ceased pursuing this particular ambition.

The way the enquirer shuffles the cards often gives the interpreter a great insight into temperament. The enquirer who gives the pack a thorough shuffle is the kind of person who does things thoroughly and wholeheartedly. This kind of person doesn't expect anything for nothing and is usually dependable.

The enquirer who hardly shuffles the pack then puts it down, while looking hopefully at the interpreter, is the kind of person who makes little effort himself yet expects maximum results. Such a person has a wishbone instead of backbone and, often, one finds that this type of person's problems arise through his or her own ineffectiveness or laziness.

This kind of person will often state that he believes in fate because that provides an easy way out of his difficulties. If he can blame his failure on fate it relieves him of the responsibility of trying: all he wants is to be told that his version of fate is going to drop all he wants in his lap.

Some people who come for readings will actually say: 'I don't really believe in all this you know.' If this happens, refuse to go on with the reading because such a person is insincere in all things.

If someone doesn't believe in the Tarot's power of delineation he shouldn't seek a Tarot reading in the first place. But, having done so, there is little point in trying to put the reader down: it is merely a mild form of ill-wishing – and we can all do without that.

Be sincere with the Tarot and it will be sincere with you. If you don't feel up to an interpretation then put it off until another time because it is inadvisable to attempt to translate a spread if you are feeling worried or unwell, but make a note of how the cards lay.

In the following pages, all references to the cards' positions relate to using the 12-card spread described here. So, if you use a different type of divinatory spread (and there are dozens to choose from), you will need to interpret the lie of the cards differently, according to the spread used.

CHAPTER 3
The Minor Arcana

In our study of the Tarot we now reach the Minor Arcana, of which the first cards in order of importance are the four Aces. These cards represent the power of the spirit acting in and binding together the four scales of each element, so each Ace has rulership over one of the elements.

The Ace of Wands
This card is the root of the powers of Fire and has its dominion in the East. It symbolises strength, speed, vigour and energy, thus it is associated with the life force, the urge of everything that is created. It is a natural, as opposed to invoked power and has rulership over all natural life and development.

In a Tarot spread, the Ace of Wands symbolises the growth or development of anything – from an idea to an undertaking. This Ace oftens falls in the first position in a divinatory spread when the enquirer feels that life is dull and flat and has lost its savour. So here, briefly, are the meanings of the Ace of Wands in a 12-card spread.

Upright in the first position: a change is imminent and the outcome will be good; reversed, the change will be enforced but, after initial difficulties, will prove beneficial. Financial changes and improved earnings are indicated if this card falls in the second place; in the third, such changes will affect the querent's relatives and he is advised not to interfere with their affairs if this card falls reversed. A member of the querent's household will move if this card falls in the fourth place; if reversed, the querent will leave his usual residence, though not necessarily permanently, so it could refer to a holiday.

In the fifth position, the beginning of a new love affair if the querent is unattached, or a welcome change in the affairs of one of his offspring if he is a parent; if reversed, the child may experience initial difficulties. The sixth position relates to health, denoting an improvement if the card is upright and that it is time for a check-up if reversed. In the seventh, a marriage or partnership is indicated although problems could be encountered if the card is reversed. Reversed or not in the eighth, it signifies the return of an old flame or friend who is out of touch.

This card has special significance in the tenth position, however it falls, for it betokens a new job or profession which will turn out well or good business prospects. In the eleventh, a current wish will be gratified although a delay of at least six weeks must be expected if the card falls reversed.

The twelfth position is also fortunate and signifies that a problem will be resolved. Help will come from an unexpected quarter and the result will be favourable although, again, a six week delay is indicated if this card falls reversed.

As has been stated, the Ace of Wands signifies new beginnings, often of a fortunate nature. The appearance of this card in a spread signifies that such changes have already been initiated, perhaps unknown to the enquirer, even if the effects are not yet obvious.

The Ace of Swords

This card is the root of the powers of Air and symbolises force that is invoked or brought into being by mankind (individually or collectively). It represents justice upholding the divine laws, and refers to wrath, punishment and affliction for transgression against these laws.

This card, therefore, has a dual meaning in a spread for it signifies both unions and enemies. So, according to the way it falls, it can be an omen of good or ill. When upright in the seventh position (which is opposite that of the enquirer since the first position always represents him or her) it signifies that the querent is about to incur enmity and, if cards of ill-omen also occupy the fourth or tenth place, this enmity will have serious consequences. When reversed in this position and fortified by good cards in the fourth and tenth, this card shows that the querent will triumph over such enmity.

Upright in the first position, this card signifies the querent's enmity towards somebody; and this person will soon let the enquirer know that he or she is aware of this enmity if the card is reversed in this place. Upright in the second, it warns of danger of a money loss, but any such loss can be recouped if the card is reversed. A planned journey could prove disappointing if this Ace is upright in the third, or cancelled altogether if reversed. Upright in the fourth, property could cause expense; reversed, a family member's fortunes will improve. Upright in the fifth means romantic difficulties; reversed, the end of an affair.

Upright in the sixth, heavy duties or extra responsibilities are denoted; reversed, the possibility of temporary unemployment. Upright in the eighth, urgent debts have to be met; reversed, others will offer financial help. Upright in the ninth, a long journey or holiday will be fraught with difficulties; reversed, the proposed trip may be cancelled. Upright in the tenth, business or career difficulties must be overcome; reversed, a change of plans or occupation brings benefits. Upright in the eleventh, a long-held wish cannot be fulfilled; reversed, the other party is not interested in the querent's wish or hope. Upright in the twelfth, the querent's activities will be restricted, perhaps by illness; reversed, restrictions will be eased or health improve.

ACE 4 CUPS.

The Ace of Cups

This card is the root of the powers of Water and corresponds to the eternal mother principle. It symbolises fertility, beauty, happiness and productiveness; it is a good augury for these things when it appears upright in a spread. It also represents the end or outcome of any matter in question and is a card of good omen whether falling or reversed.

Upright in any position, this Ace signifies conviviality, good news and rejoicing. When reversed, it presages an alteration in one's life that could be the start of a new enterprise, inspired labour (usually of a creative kind) or the beginning of an important love affair. Wherever this card falls, it has a happy significance, but there are certain positions in a 12-card spread where this card's appearance qualifies what will happen.

In the fifth or eleventh place, the Ace of Cups heralds the beginning of a new love affair of significance. In the second, it indicates rejoicing over a monetary gain, which could be substantial. In the fourth, a beautiful and permanent home will be secured. In the seventh, a happy marriage or successful debut in public life is promised. In the tenth, the querent's ambitions will be realised.

This card has a special significance if it falls in the first position because it denotes that the querent will receive what is sometimes known as the blessings of the gods. In other words, great happiness will come his way because he will have earned it through meritorious conduct in the past and is thus due to receive his just reward.

The Ace of Pentacles
This card is the root of the powers of Earth and has dominion over mundane matters of all kinds. It stands for materialism, gains, work, wealth and power. When not reversed in a spread, this card is a good omen and shows the successful outcome of any question concerned with material matters, ambitions or personal power. But when reversed, it warns the querent that he is following an illusion or that he is on the wrong path which, if not abandoned, can lead to the negation of that which is actually desired.

When upright in the first position this card is a good omen, indicating financial gain from a new enterprise; when reversed, it signifies a small monetary gain or, where such is likely, a small legacy. This latter is more probable if the reversed cards fall in the eighth position which also denotes financial gain. In the following readings, note that when the card is reversed it indicates that any monetary gains promised will be smaller than if the card falls upright.

Reversed in the second position, the Ace of Pentacles signifies that money the querent has earned will come to him. Upright or reversed in the third, this card denotes that relatives could offer financial help or make a gift of money to the querent. In the fourth, property or family matters will result in financial gain; in the fifth, a windfall of some kind is indicated as it denotes unexpected money. A new job with a higher salary is signified by the sixth position; and financial gain for the querent or his or her partner, perhaps as a result of an old debt being repaid, if this card falls in the seventh.

In the ninth place, money comes through the settlement of a contract or legal matter; in the tenth, business success is indicated. In the eleventh, a stroke of money luck is indicated by the upright card and extra cash through a friend is denoted by the reversed card. A successful resolution to a financial problem is signified by the twelfth position as help will come from an outside agency.

These, then, are the major meanings of the Tarot Aces in a divinatory spread, but it must not be assumed that the use of the Tarot pack is solely for purposes of prediction. It means far more than that and is a pictorial record of the 78 steps any serious student of the occult must be prepared to learn before his powers can be used wisely.

Between knowledge and wisdom there is a great gap: we can all have knowledge of something but to have the wisdom to use what we know is a different matter altogether. Wisdom comes from experience of the trials and vicissitudes of life, from which no one is exempt. The student occultist, indeed, often has to endure more since he must be able to pass on the knowledge and wisdom gained through his own experiences.

Anyone can learn to read the Tarot as knowledge is free and open to all, but to understand the true wisdom it contains one must learn from life's experiences – for this is what it signifies.

The Twos

In a spread, the exoteric meanings of the four Twos of the Minor Arcana are simple, but in the study of the inner symbolism of the Tarot – its more magical aspect – the Twos represent conflicting forces.

The whole universe is dualistic: there are positives and negatives – light and dark, birth and death; there are good and bad deeds, good and bad consequences; there is war and peace, love and hate. Everything has its reverse side, the other side of the Two. In other words, in all things there are twin forces at work. Yet, in the final analysis, it is up to us.

We all know, or sense, when we are going wrong or doing wrong and, if we perpetuate this, so much the worse for us. After all, we always have a choice and can bring the reverse side of the card into operation if we so wish. Therefore, the simple law of the Twos is to do what is right because, eventually, no matter what may occur in the meantime, the end itself must come out right if we do.

Bearing this point in mind, we will now consider the divinatory meanings of the Twos of the Minor Arcana and, in particular, those positions in a 12-card spread where these cards have especial significance. All the Twos have a bearing on romantic and financial issues, so may signify either in a spread.

The Two of Cups
This card can indicate reciprocated love; but when reversed denotes love that is discouraged or rejected. Either way up it represents wealth, but also miserliness. This card often depicts people who, though truly loved, are suspicious that they are loved for their money or possessions.

This card is a happy augury of a fortunate and reciprocated love affair if it falls upright in the fifth, seventh or eleventh position; and is an omen of a yet unknown but important romance for the querent if upright in the first position. If reversed in any of these positions, romance is ill-omened and, if in the seventh, an existing partnership is at risk.

Also associated with wealth, the Two of Cups upright in the second or eighth position is indicative of a monetary rather than an emotional gain. When reversed in the first, fifth or eleventh, it denotes the querent's miserliness and this may refer to emotional miserliness if in the first. In any other position in a spread, this card can have a helpful, though not very strong influence.

The Two of Pentacles
In any spread this card warns querents that they may not be able to establish money or love affairs satisfactorily; when reversed, however, an unexpected happening will settle the financial or romantic issue, for better or worse depending on the querent's personal circumstances.

Since the Tarot speaks of the future and this is a lunar card, it signifies that the querent will experience financial difficulties after the next

New Moon if it falls upright in the first or second position. If reversed in either of these, some form of financial help is indicated although this may not be sufficient to solve the querent's problem entirely in certain cases.

There is one other position in which this card is significant and that is the fifth. Whether upright or reversed, I have found that it portends a monetary gain when placed here; in any other position in a spread, however, this card loses its importance.

The Two of Wands

This card warns of troubles or crossings in love, or of unforeseen obstacles to a business enterprise. Reversed, it signifies the speedy receipt of a communication that settles either matter favourably. This card usually denotes those people who can't make up their minds about romance or finance and need to have such decisions made for them.

If upright in the fifth or eleventh position, this card does not augur well for affairs of the heart; unforeseen obstacles are presaged if it is upright in the first or seventh place, especially in financial matters. The most fortunate position for this card to fall is reversed in the third as this denotes a favourable communication concerning whichever of these matters – love or money – is uppermost in the querent's mind at the time of the reading.

The Two of Swords

To my mind, this card is the most important of the four Twos as it has interesting connotations, both in a spread and from an occult point of view. When this card falls upright in a spread, it portends amiability and friendship or, in some instances, an overture of peace from a former enemy or a gift that comes as a peace-offering. However, if reversed, it signifies that such advances from a former adversary may be founded upon deceit and guile.

The most significant positions for this card are the first and seventh because its influence is strongest in these and, if it is also reversed, the querent is strongly advised to beware of deception and guile from an antagonist, despite any friendly overtures such a person may make.

The relationships most emphasised by this card are close family friendships in the fourth position; lovers in the fifth or eleventh; distant relatives or in-laws in the third or ninth; and partners and business associates when in the seventh.

The Threes

Hidden in the Major and Minor Arcana of the Tarot are all the lost secrets of the ages, if we could but fathom them. Besides being associated with the trinity, the Threes also stand for the physical, mental, spiritual and astral planes. These correspondences may not be immediately obvious unless one simplifies them as follows.

The Three of Pentacles is concerned with material things, hence corresponds to the physical plane; the Three of Wands is a mental card because it denotes optimism or hopefulness; the Three of Cups corresponds to the spiritual and is a success card as nothing daunts the spirit; while the Three of Swords stands for the astral plane on which all that is created by the power of thought, whether for good or bad, has its counterpart.

The Three of Swords

This card is malign in meaning, whether reversed or not, because it signifies hatred, strife and disunion; separation or divorce; disillusionment; and fraud or lies on the part of the enquirer.

When reversed, the troubles that this card portends can be put down to the misjudgement or behaviour of the enquirer, especially if it falls in the first position. When in the seventh, the fault lies with the enquirer's loved one or partner, who may desire a separation. If this card falls in the fourth or tenth place, such a separation seems inevitable; in the fifth, it betokens the end of a love affair.

In any other position in a spread, this Three loses much of its malign influence although, if it falls in the second place and is opposed by an unfortunate card in the eighth, it signifies money loss or fraud through the actions of a business partner or associate.

The Three of Wands

This card has a predictive aspect which is very encouraging, whether upright or reversed. It indicates good fortune wherever it falls, but especially in the first, second or tenth position and, when upright, denotes wealth and renown.

In its reversed aspect, this card represents the trier – the person who is prepared to work to achieve his ambitions. So, this Three is one of the many cards that can only be interpreted according to the kind of person the enquirer is and whether or not he or she is likely to make use of the opportunities presaged by this card. It is an excellent omen for some people but should be wholly discounted if the querent is someone with no special abilities or ambitions.

Wealth is relative, but when this card falls in the second position, it promises unexpected money; upright in the tenth, it indicates fame or renown, and the money associated with this. When reversed, especially in the first, sixth or tenth place, it advises the querent that the time is ripe to lay the foundations of a successful career or business venture.

The Three of Cups
This card promises success, often accompanied by fame; the satisfactory termination of any enterprise engaged upon; and fulfilled hopes if it falls upright in the first, tenth or eleventh position in a spread.

If reversed in any of these positions, however, it indicates the negation of such hopes, particularly when reversed in the tenth position. This Three not only signifies fame for those with the ability to attract it by their talents and enterprise but also that unfortunate sister to fame – notoriety. It is very difficult to win the adulation of the world but all too easy to get publicity which results in smears and condemnation, so this card must be interpreted only according to its position and the querent's circumstances.

The Three of Pentacles
When this card falls upright in a spread, it signifies a business proposal or undertaking but, when reversed, is unlikely to have much

significance. So, if this card falls in the second or tenth place, the querent could soon be invited to participate in a business venture that will prove profitable but, if reversed in the fourth or seventh position, nothing would be likely to come of such a deal.

This Three must be considered in relation to the querent's circumstances at the time of the reading because, if he is enjoying a fortunate period and the card falls upright, the business proposal indicated will have successful results. If, however, he is undergoing one of those exasperating periods when everything seems to go wrong and this card falls reversed in any of the positions stated, he should not pin high hopes on any such business arrangement because it also signifies that his present ideas or methods are wrong and need revising if he is to succeed.

Whether in business or anything else, everybody has periods when things seem to go dreadfully wrong: bad luck, lack of money, disputes and separations from those we love all seem to go hand in hand. The period of such a run of misfortune is usually three months or three years (signified by the Three of Pentacles), with the fourth month or year seeing gradual improvements all round. From then on, better luck mounts as the pressure of events slowly eases. So, if you have been experiencing such a period, take heart if the Three of Pentacles turns up in a spread for it can signify that such a period is coming to an end.

The Fours

To stand four-square is the secret behind the Fours in the Minor Arcana. Standing four-square is itself an occult term, for it denotes the four points of the compass we call North, South, East and West; the Wheel of Ezekiel has four phases, those of the bull, the lion, the eagle and man; there are four Watchtowers of Earth and four Watchers in each of them; there are four seasons in the year and four lunar phases.

The square, or difficult aspect in astrology, has four equal sides and usually signifies some difficulty that has to be overcome. Thus it is with the cards numbered Four in the Minor Arcana, each has its contradictory meaning according to whether it falls upright or reversed in a spread: that which was easy can become difficult, yet trials can yield to better things. This is the arcanum of the Tarot Fours and should be borne in mind when interpreting a spread, for it is not enough to know just the divinatory meanings of the cards, each must be considered according to its placement and the querent's circumstances at the time of the reading.

The Four of Pentacles

As this card relates to money matters, its predictive meaning is simple. When it falls upright in the first, fifth or eleventh position, it denotes forthcoming social amusements, parties and the entertainment of guests. However, should this card fall reversed in the second or eighth position, it signifies that the entertainment of others may involve the querent in excessive or pointless expense.

Money has its own arcanum; the ebb and flow of finance responds to some unusual laws and any occult method of attracting money luck always stresses two points. One is that one must give in order to receive, and the other is that one must set faith, wit and hands to work to obtain it. It is certainly true that the good spender never seems to lack money for long whereas the over-careful person never seems to have any financial windfalls or money luck.

The Four of Cups

When this card falls reversed in the first, fifth or eleventh position, it means that the querent's love affair is in serious danger of going wrong. When upright in one of these positions, however, it signifies a new and pleasant association which may or may not lead to love, according to the degree of affinity between the enquirer and the other person.

Here, it is necessary to stress that the first and fifth positions are important for men as far as this particular card is concerned, while for women the first and eleventh positions are more significant. Also, any romantic difficulties encountered are likely to arise through outside influences, perhaps a change in personal circumstances for the enquirer or the beloved, or the interference or invervention of another person.

The Four of Wands

When upright in a spread, this card promises gaiety, pleasure, enjoyable company and the love of congenial friends, particularly if this card falls in the first, fifth or eleventh position. When reversed in the first, fifth, tenth or eleventh position, however, it betokens impediments to the success of an important project or hope and a generally unsympathetic atmosphere.

In the first or tenth place, this usually applies to a business project or something that could diminish the success of the enquirer. When reversed in the fifth or eleventh, though, this card must be taken to mean that the enquirer's love affairs, friendships, social life or personal hopes are under a cloud that will take time to disperse.

The Four of Swords

When it falls upright in a spread, this card denotes mysticism, occultism, religion or voluntary seclusion. It has to be upright in the ninth position for the first three definitions to apply and upright in the twelfth to signify voluntary seclusion. If this card should fall reversed, it stands for disaster, loneliness and compulsory seclusion, perhaps allied to ruin and, in extreme cases, a prison cell.

The significant places for the reversed card to fall should, therefore, be noted. In the first position it heralds a disaster; in the fifth and eleventh, loneliness; and in the twelfth, compulsory seclusion. In any other position in a 12-card spread, this card loses its import.

The Four of Swords is the saddest of all the Four cards and is the reverse aspect of the Four of Wands; indeed, these two cards often turn up together in a spread. Comedy and tragedy often follow one another in life and the Four of Swords brings to bear the whole four-square confining influence. It is a card which represents a person of great abilities, even great attainments, but who can bring about self-ruin.

So, when upright in the correct position in a spread, it indicates that the enquirer has reached the stage of mental development when occult secrets are not only needed but can be of practical help. When reversed in the positions designated, however, it is a warning that the querent's present way of life, thought and deed is leading towards disaster, which could be of major or minor proportions according to the factors involved.

The Fives

It has been written that love conquers all but, like all generalisations, analysis proves this false. Love plays a great part in human life and our enjoyment of it, yet love cannot be trapped, demanded as a right or won as a conquest.

The Five of Wands

Love can only be earned, which is the underlying theme of the Five of Wands. In a divinatory spread, this card falling in the fifth position, marking the progress of a love affair, or in the seventh, indicating the hope of a union or marriage, has the following meanings.

When upright in either of those positions, this Five denotes a love affair which will triumph over any obstacles that seem to threaten its successful culmination. When reversed, however, it has an entirely different meaning for it warns of unreciprocated love or even tragic love. If, in addition to being reversed in the fifth or seventh place, it is opposed by a card of sad omen from the first or eleventh position, it foretells illicit love – one that is prohibited, unlawful or forbidden in any sense or at any level.

The Five of Cups

When falling upright, and fortified by harmonious cards, the Five of Cups heralds the happy conclusion to a love affair or, if the querent is unattached, marriage, often coupled with a gift or monetary gain. If this card is reversed, it signifies the early receipt of unexpected news or the unexpected arrival of a friend.

For love questions, the fifth and eleventh positions are important. This card in either of those places, fortified by a card of good omen in the opposite position, signifies gratified and reciprocated love. Marriage is promised if this card falls in the seventh position with a well-omened card in the first. If this Five falls reversed in the first, third or ninth position in a 12-card spread, it denotes the arrival of much wanted news or a visit from a friend in the near future.

The Five of Pentacles

The appearance of the Five of Pentacles in a spread, especially when occupying the first or second position, denotes an unhoped-for sum of money that can compensate for previous losses. However, when reversed, it denotes a small monetary gain that may lead to anxiety or legal difficulties.

To those who realise that the ancient cards of the Tarot are more than mere fortune-telling devices, an eerie note of warning sounds when this card turns up in a spread. This card is supposed to have two lords sharing rulership over it. One of these is the power known as the Lord of Material Trouble who has been appointed to wipe the self-satisfied smile off humanity's face by means of certain material afflictions.

Such difficulties include loss of money or worldy status, poverty, hardship and trial – all experiences that are suffered on the material plane. Thus, the sufferer experiences a lack of all that makes life easy and pleasant, except for one important factor – he will always have affection, perhaps even great love, to lighten the dark road he must follow for a while.

The Five of Swords
The most ill-omened Five in the Tarot, though, is the Five of Swords, no matter where it falls in a spread, and the enquirer should be put on his guard by seeing it. That is the value of the Tarot; it can issue warnings so that steps can be taken to ameliorate any potential dangers or difficulties. However, whether reversed or the right way up, this card signifies sorrow, loss and the triumph of one's enemies.

It is a warning wherever it appears in a spread, but particularly in the seventh or twelfth position. When in the seventh, the potential enemy is likely to be someone the enquirer is aware of and the danger lies in his personal life; so this could refer to a rival in his marriage or affairs of the heart. In the twelfth, the enemy is a secret one, someone unknown to the querent, and the greatest risk concerns business rivalry, treachery or confidence trickery. In some cases, it could relate to burglaries, especially when this Five falls reversed in the twelfth.

These, then, are the exoteric or outer meanings of the Fives. Their inner meaning is associated with the five-pointed star, the pentagram, which can be depicted two ways: with one point upward (the pentagram of man), or with two points uppermost (the pentagram of power). The first represents man himself – the head is the apex and the four limbs are accommodated by the other points of the star. The latter, representing man's urgent desire to achieve his ends through whatever means can be employed, accommodates a goat's head – two horns in the uppermost points and ears and chin in the other three – signifying Capricorn, ruler of the tenth house of the zodiac, the house associated with individual status, ambition and desire for power.

Of course, ambitions are laudable, especially if attained by merit and fair dealing: the goat must climb. But we must climb rightly, as responsible and conscientious people, considering those we may injure on the way up and learning to say no to ourselves when we are in danger of being unfair. If we do this, the benefits of three of the Minor Arcana Fives will be felt; but if we let our urges and desires control us, we will suffer from the reversal of these cards by falling under the illusion of the goat pentacle and the dreadful portents of the Five of Swords will be fulfilled.

The Sixes

In the Minor Arcana of the Tarot, the Sixes have been called the serpents, perhaps because if one studies the shapes of the figures or writes them together, they form serpentine loops. Serpent power is manifold, sometimes representing wisdom, other times healing and, in certain myths, it has sexual connotations. In Tarot readings, however, it relates to those events in people's lives that eventually enmesh them, whether or not they have consciously contributed to the result.

Most of us have experienced such a situation. One event, perhaps of no importance in itself, leads to another; other people become involved and react with each other; eventually, someone else gets caught up in the act, often unwittingly or unwillingly, and with unhelpful consequences. So, if we look at the exoteric meanings of the Sixes in a divinatory spread, we will get some idea of what the coils of the serpent can do.

The Six of Wands

This card, when falling upright in the first, fifth or eleventh position of a 12-card spread, denotes the complete reversal or failure of a project. And, when reversed in any of the positions mentioned, it denotes vain and fruitless striving and desires. Elsewhere in a spread, this card loses much of its importance and simply refers to minor disappointments.

The lack of success portended by this Six will be due to the influence of a third party whose strong personality is such that failure is almost inevitable, especially in any matter close to the heart of the enquirer. In any significant position in a spread, then, this card warns the querent that he will suffer defeat at the hands of a rival in a matter that is important to him at the time of the reading.

The Six of Swords
The predictive meaning of the Six of Swords is a voyage over water or the arrival of a traveller or messenger and, if reversed in the second or eighth position, gain from an unexpected quarter. If the upright card falls in the ninth position, it signifies a voyage or long-distance travel for the querent; in the third place it denotes the arrival of an unexpected visitor or news of some importance.

This card depicts a journey over water and, in all arcane matters, water represents an emotional element, as do tears. So another interpretation of this Six is that tears will be shed over some event or news received by the enquirer.

The Six of Pentacles
When the Six of Pentacles is upright, especially in the second or eighth position, it denotes disputes over money. This could refer to a debt for which payment is demanded; a loan that must be repaid or

legal action will ensue; or, if money is owed to the enquirer, he may experience difficulty in getting it without resorting to legal action and, even then, may lose out.

However, this card has a more hopeful significance when reversed in a spread, especially in the first, second or eighth position. It then portends unexpected cash resources becoming available to the enquirer which will enable him to overcome his financial difficulty at the time of the reading.

The Six of Cups
This card is one of the most puzzling cards in the Minor Arcana because it has no clearly defined meaning of its own and can only be interpreted according to the cards with which it is associated in a spread, especially that which opposes it. When this Six falls upright, the cards that accompany it will refer to actions and events that took place in the past but, if this card is reversed, it signifies that these things have not yet come to pass but will do so very shortly.

This Six often appears in conjunction with the card representing the querent in a spread and, when it does, I have found that it usually indicates an obsession with the past or that the enquirer has a particular bee in his bonnet concerning some incident in the past.

So much for the individual meanings of the Sixes in a divinatory spread but, should all four appear in the same spread, then their combined influence will come to bear. Thus, if all four Sixes follow one another in a spread, no matter in what order, it signifies that the querent has reached the point in life where past and future meet. All the cards numbered Six have strong associations with the past and indicate that the necessary consequences are about to take effect in the enquirer's life.

These effects represent the harvest of deeds done in the past and can be beneficial or otherwise depending on the nature of the acts which triggered them off. And, should one of the Sixes fall on the card representing the querent, it will indicate in which particular area of life these consequences will be felt, according to the meaning of this particular card.

But, however the cards fall, the serpentine Sixes foretell events that are beyond the power of the enquirer to control, at least temporarily. They indicate occurrences that are inevitable because the enquirer has become entangled – however unwittingly or unwillingly – in the serpent coils of past actions or events.

The Sevens

Seven is usually considered a fortunate number and many people attach spiritual importance to it; certainly it is a number which holds a peculiar fascination for many people. There are numerous biblical references to the number seven: the seven angels with the seven trumpets in Revelations, for example, and the seven-horned beast. Religion has incorporated it in the seven-branched candlestick of the Hebrew faith and the Christian Coptic cross.

If four sevens, each facing a different point of the compass, are joined together in the middle this produces a swastika: a very ancient sacred symbol which was regarded as signifying good fortune or well-being before its unfortunate political associations caused it to fall into disrepute. Embellish this figure by giving the sevens two top bars of equal length instead of one and the Coptic cross is formed.

There are also the seven days in the week, the seven ages of man, seven seas, seven ancient planets, seven ruling angels and seven keys to knowledge, just to quote a few examples. So, with all this arcanum concerning the number seven, it is easy to see why it is regarded as a mystic number and why it should be considered as important in the Minor Arcana of the Tarot.

The Seven of Cups

This card portends an unexpected stroke of good luck or success that was not expected and, even when reversed, implies beneficial conditions. Wherever this card appears in a spread, it presages coming good fortune and, should it fall in the fifth or eleventh position in a 12-card spread, denotes success in love.

The swastika is one of the oldest sacred symbols in the world and represents one of the keys to power: power through wisdom.

Esoterically, the Seven of Cups represents the eastern leg of the swastika, signifying occult or psychic power. (That, incidentally, is how the idea arose that the seventh son/daughter of a seventh son/daughter had natural psychic gifts.) So, in a divinatory spread, this card signifies that occult or psychic powers will help the querent to attain happiness and success.

The Seven of Wands
This is concerned with financial good fortune and denotes business dealings or transactions of any kind in which money is involved. This card has most influence when falling in the second, fourth, sixth and tenth positions. When upright in the second place, it denotes an increase in money or earnings, even perhaps a legacy; in the fourth, the omen is fortunate for business deals connected with real estate; in the sixth, it indicates a promotion and increased earnings; and in the tenth, great business success or career advancement allied with monetary gain.

When reversed in a spread, however, it warns against undue optimism as the querent's business affairs are about to reach a turning point. So, if this card falls reversed in any of the positions mentioned, their reversed meanings could apply and the querent is advised to avoid any important business transactions for a period of at least three months after the reading, if at all possible, and to consider any proposals very carefully before commitment to a change of career direction.

The Seven of Pentacles
This card is also concerned with financial matters and is always a favourable omen if it falls upright in a spread. The most important positions for this card to fall are the first or second and, when upright in either of these, it signifies a money gain or gift of some kind but, if reversed, it indicates financial worries of a temporary nature.

Yet, even if this card does fall reversed in a spread, it should not be regarded as a card of ill-omen for any financial difficulties will be of a temporary nature only because this Seven signifies an upward trend in the querent's affairs. It heralds a period of improved fortunes and should, therefore, be considered as a fortunate card wherever and however it falls in a spread.

The Seven of Swords
This card, when upright in a spread, is an assurance of brighter financial and business prospects, especially in the first or tenth position. When reversed in these positions, it signifies that the querent's personal rivals or business opponents are at present in a strong position. Should this card fall in the ninth place, whether upright or reversed, it often denotes that the enquirer is contemplating some form of legal action and warns that he or she would be better off settling the matter out of court, cutting losses rather than going to law, as the outcome of an action would not be satisfactory.

The Seven of Swords also symbolises the seven armed powers that fight on man's behalf. So, if the querent's cause is just, these heavenly powers will come to his aid when he least expects it. Then, no matter what he or his rivals do, the tables will be turned on his enemies because his case has gone before a heavenly court whose judgement is not fallible and where no biased or false witnesses can prevail. This is the connexion with the swastika, the key to power through wisdom, for this refers not only to man's wisdom but also that of a higher and more just power which offers help when we least expect it if our cause is just and we appeal to this higher court for judgement.

The Eights

Eight is sometimes called the number of Fate and is associated with Justice, the eighth card of the Major Arcana. The Eights of the Minor Arcana are fateful cards, too, and often turn up in a divinatory spread when fate is about to take a hand in the querent's life. Eight is a number of final decision and is often irrevocable in effect. It is also a number of termination, meaning that it can bring to an end a run of either good or bad luck.

Everything in life has a terminating point after which circumstances are changed for better or for worse, and it is such points in life that are represented by the Eights of the Minor Arcana. It is essential, therefore, to interpret the fall of these cards according to the personal circumstances of the querent at the time of the reading or it will be impossible to predict the future outcome.

The Eight of Cups
This card marks the culmination of courtship and stands for a happy marriage thereafter. It is a happy augury in any spread because it signifies the esteem in which the querent is held by a friend or lover. Even when reversed, this card still holds out the same promise

although qualified by the warning that disputes, difficulties or friction could delay the emotional happiness implicit in this Eight.

This card can be regarded, therefore, as a fortunate omen for the success of a love affair, especially if it falls in the first, fifth or eleventh position. I have found that the first and fifth are the most important for men; and the first and eleventh the most significant if the querent is a woman.

The Eight of Pentacles

This card denotes prosperity or otherwise, according to how it falls in a spread. When upright, it signifies a well-ordered, tranquil period coupled with prosperity, especially if this card falls in the second, tenth or eleventh position. It is well-omened in other positions, too, but not so strongly.

Should the card fall reversed in the tenth position, it denotes strife and disorder in the querent's life; reversed in the eleventh, a hope that he has set his heart on is likely to fail; reversed in the second, it indicates that money difficulties are on the way although these can be overcome in time. When reversed in the first position, however, it warns the querent that money luck is being spoilt by his or her mental attitude and it is necessary to take stock if the personal financial situation is to be improved.

The Eight of Wands

The significance of the Eight of Wands varies according to its position in a spread. When upright, however, it can always be regarded as a good omen as it denotes that the querent can achieve his aims or effect desired changes. The two most influential positions for this card to fall are upright in the seventh, where it signifies a union or partnership with an upstanding and straightforward person of the opposite sex, and reversed in the seventh, where it warns of worry or deception due to a person of the opposite sex and can be regarded as a warning in a love affair.

As this card has such varied meanings, I will list briefly the significance of the Eight of Wands when upright in each of the 12 positions of a divinatory spread. In the first, achievement of a personal aim; second, a monetary gain; third, inspiration leading to success; fourth, a gain in property; fifth, success in a love affair or the birth of a desired child; sixth, gain through or security of an occupational position; seventh, a union or partnership; eighth, gain through insurance or a legacy; ninth, an unexpected but fortunate long-distance journey; tenth, achievement of ambition; eleventh, coming fulfilment of a personal wish; and twelfth, defeat of a rival or enemy.

When the Eight of Wands falls reversed in any position, the upright meaning must be reversed for it signifies that the coming changes will be of an unfavourable nature.

The Eight of Swords
This card can be regarded as one of the most ill-omened cards in the pack for it signifies quarrels, rivalry and illness when upright in a spread, and a calamity or accident resulting in bloodshed when reversed. It is a very hard card to interpret in a spread because it can denote almost anything from a lovers' tiff, and subsequent digestive upset, to a fatal accident: it all depends on the querent, as well as the lie of the other cards in the spread which may modify its interpretation and the interpreter.

However, this card does have its more hopeful aspect. Basically, it denotes the lowest point in one cycle and matters must, therefore, improve once this depressing episode is over. Each of us must pass through ordeals at certain points in our lives from the moment of birth – the first ordeal – to the moment of death – the ordeal we all fail to pass. There are eight of these points in all, and the six that lie between birth and death are marked by the Eights of the Minor Arcana.

These are all times of initiation on this plane – times when we are paying off karma or learning a lesson through the events taking place in our daily lives. The fateful Eights of the Tarot bring the past into the present and future, thus ensuring that we reap what we have sown: our past deeds crystallise into present and future events for, in the last analysis, we are judged on our merits and our past actions can blight or enhance our future.

The Nines

Most people have an inner awareness that they can be blessed or cursed. Few understand, however, that they can be blessed or cursed, as the case may be, through circumstances arising from their own actions. We are the architects of our fate and of our destruction because we have the free will to choose. When we choose the wrong way, we know this deep down inside ourselves; we also know that, one day, there must be retribution.

Yet, it is always easier to blame outside circumstances than it is to blame ourselves. We can retire behind the imaginary victimisation of a curse far more easily than we can admit that we brought a train of ill-fortune to ourselves because we acted selfishly, foolishly or even criminally. But curses, like blessings, come as a result of our past actions; they are what is due to us and so, come what may, we must work out our own destruction or salvation.

This point is aptly illustrated by the Nines of the Minor Arcana. Two of them, the Nine of Cups and the Nine of Pentacles, are cards of good omen. The first signifies success in the matter enquired about and the second denotes material gain. But, just as there is a good side to the Nines, so there is an evil one. The Nine of Swords and the Nine of Wands are grim warnings and come as reminders of past misdeeds for they represent retribution. And, should both these Nines appear in the same spread, it warns the enquirer that whatever he has in mind should be abandoned at once or a trail of misfortune will ensue, especially if both cards fall on, or next to the significator (the card representing the querent in a spread).

The Nine of Wands and the Nine of Swords

The Nine of Wands implies underhand dealings, treachery to others and disloyalty to one's own when it lies with the Nine of Swords because this latter card reinforces the omens. The Nine of Swords warns of disillusionment accompanied by suspicion, hatred and the break-up of all that may have been acquired as a result of wrong actions or motives.

These two cards (whether singly or together) are apt to feature prominently in spreads of people with obstinate and selfish dispositions. They usually warn of emotional entanglements and dishonesty in business or financial dealings and can be regarded as cards of retribution. If their warnings go unheeded, powers higher than those of man will ensure that the person concerned will pay the full price: what he has will turn to dust and ashes; what he loses will never be regained. The law of retribution is inexorable, yet only we can set it in motion.

In direct contrast to these ill-omened Nines are the Nine of Cups and the Nine of Pentacles. These two cards indicate that the querent is about to be rewarded for past efforts made or for good deeds done and both can, therefore, be regarded as deserved blessings.

The Nine of Pentacles

In a divinatory spread, the Nine of Pentacles denotes quite a substantial income which comes as a reward for past efforts, or the proper application of abilities. Without such application, even with occult aid and knowledge, no lasting benefit can accrue, so it is important to consider the nature of the querent if this card appears in a spread in order to judge whether or not the material gains promised by this card will have a lasting effect.

Even when reversed, this is still a well-omened card although the benefits it implies will take longer to accumulate and there may be obstacles along the way which will have to be overcome before its promises can be fulfilled. The most significant positions for this card to fall are upright in the first, second and fifth, as these indicate that financial gains and success are imminent; yet it is a well-omened card wherever and however it falls.

The Nine of Cups

This card has a very simple and fortunate meaning for it signifies the gratification of wishes, and is a good omen whenever it appears in a spread. Even if reversed, it still denotes the fulfilment of wishes although these may be delayed temporarily and is, therefore, often referred to as the wish card. Again, like the Nine of Pentacles, this card signifies the rewards of past good actions and symbolises deserved blessings.

The Nine of Cups is one of the luckiest cards in the pack and its good effects apply no matter what the nature of the wish may be because it is the card which symbolises good fortune and fulfilled love. It implies the lasting happiness which is earned rather than a flash of good luck that can fade as quickly as it appears. It is, therefore, an excellent augury whenever this card appears in a spread.

We all experience dark years when one thing after another goes wrong, when nothing but struggle and disappointment seem to fall to our lot and life is very hard to bear. Such times are sent to try us, literally, and if we emerge bloody but unbowed, surviving the hard times and learning from them without resorting to selfishness, deceit or dishonesty, then we will earn our just rewards: we will gain the blessing that the Nine of Cups has to offer those who deserve them.

The Tens

In considering the Tens of the Minor Arcana, we must bear in mind that they are associated with three Major Arcana cards: No. 0, the Fool; No. 1, the Magician; and No. 10, the Wheel of Fortune.

As the number 10 is composed of 1 (the Magician) and 0 (the Fool), it follows that the Tens signify a turn of events which can be for better or worse, according to how a situation is handled. If we act foolishly, the Wheel of Fortune will turn adversely; if we are wise, it will turn in our favour. Above all, it is the way we think (No. 1) before we act which will decide the outcome.

The whole arcanum of the Tens depends on how the querent handles the events described by the cards and any Ten, therefore, has most significance if it falls on the card representing the querent in a spread. Here, then, are brief meanings for the Tens of the Minor Arcana when falling directly on the significator:

The *Ten of Cups* represents the home and the esteem in which the querent is held by his associates. When reversed, this card stands for family friction.

The *Ten of Wands* indicates travel or unfamiliar places. If reversed, it denotes that travel may have unfortunate consequences.

The *Ten of Swords* is always a card of evil omen for it portends unhappiness, depression and material privations. When reversed, it indicates that a small gain may precede the main effects which may, in fact, arise as a direct result of the gain.

The *Ten of Pentacles* links directly with the Wheel of Fortune and, whether reversed or not, signifies an unexpected monetary gain.

All the Tens have most significance when falling directly on the card of the enquirer because of the importance attached to the way he or she handles the situation depicted, yet these cards do, of course, have other divinatory meanings and other significant positions.

The Ten of Cups

This card is an important augury because it promises that happiness is on the way, no matter where it falls in a spread. This card usually turns up when some unexpected or even long-awaited happiness is about to enter the querent's life. If it falls in the first or third position, it signifies that the good fortune is imminent, but will be delayed if the card lies in the seventh or eleventh place. In the fifth position, it indicates that chance will soon play its part and lead to the querent hearing of happiness to come.

This card does not, by itself, usually describe what particular source of happiness is likely to come the querent's way. But it does, nevertheless, portend coming good fortune even if this should be delayed owing to the fall of the card in a spread.

The Ten of Wands
This card represents an unfamiliar town or environment and often turns up in a spread when the enquirer is about to undertake a journey, move house or even change his or her job if this entails a move. It denotes short trips and long journeys, holidays and emigration.

When upright in the third or ninth position, such travel will turn out well, as will the querent's prospects. When reversed in these positions, however, the querent is advised to cancel or postpone any travel plans. If the querent is considering emigration and this card falls in the tenth position, he or she would be wise to go if the card is upright, but is advised to stay if it is reversed. In any position other than those mentioned, this Ten loses much of its import and usually refers to ideas rather than events.

The Ten of Swords

This is a card of ill-omen yet, even so, it does offer a ray of hope. It is the darkness before the dawn and when it appears in the first position in a spread symbolises the enquirer at lowest ebb. But when things are at their worst – and only then – the tide must turn, as must the Wheel of Fortune.

One must be utterly vanquished before a rise can begin, which is the meaning of the supine figure depicted on this card. The person concerned has hit rock bottom and there is nowhere lower for him to go, so the only way to go is up.

The Ten of Pentacles

This represents a sum of money coming to the enquirer even when the card is reversed although it then denotes that the gain will be smaller. The first, second and fifth positions are the most fortunate for this card to fall in as they indicate certain gain. In the seventh, the spouse or business partner of the querent will be the beneficiary; in the twelfth, the money will come in the form of a gift; elsewhere in a spread, this card simply indicates a future monetary gain.

As already stated, the Ten of Pentacles relates directly to the Wheel of Fortune which is ever-turning, alternately bringing benefits or reprisals. So if this card appears in a spread, it indicates that the Wheel is about to turn in the querent's favour. Thus, if the Ten falls in one of the positions mentioned, the unexpected gain is imminent and, if it falls anywhere else in a spread, there will be a short delay before benefiting from the Wheel's turn.

The Pages

There are four Pages in the Minor Arcana and they correspond to the Jacks in a pack of playing cards. They are sometimes referred to as Knaves because they were regarded as signifying knavish tricks and intentions in the matters pertaining to the suits they ruled; thus the Knave of Cups referred to love questions; the Knave of Wands to commerce; Knave of Pentacles to money luck; and Knave of Swords to enemies or rivals.

However, I prefer to call these cards Pages because they represent young people, meaning children or young adolescents who are still under parental control, as well as young (new) ideas or a new situation – anything new is young in the sense that it hasn't yet reached maturity. So, if a Page appears in a spread, it can indicate that the querent is young in heart, experience or outlook.

These cards can also represent the thoughts of people, messages, gossip and minor news. In fact, the Pages have so many different meanings that they can clutter up or confuse a spread. It is advisable, therefore, to decide which particular aspect of the Pages you are concerned with before shuffling and laying out the cards.

If none of the matters mentioned is of great import to the querent at the time of the reading, the Pages can even be removed from the pack before the cards are shuffled as they may otherwise occupy spaces to which they give no meaning. But, if the question does concern children or any of the other matters mentioned, they should be left in the pack and interpreted only in relation to the particular facet that concerns the querent.

The Page of Cups
This card represents female children or young girls, loving thoughts or a young person of either sex who could be the bearer of a message, possibly even a love letter. Alternatively, if the querent's question concerns family matters, this card implies a birth in the family

because it represents the infant. If this card falls reversed, it is a warning of trickery, especially in love affairs.

The Page of Wands
Usually symbolises a female child or can signify someone who brings news about a relative of the querent. It also signifies friendly thoughts and, if the querent's question concerns money, reassures him that his financial interests are well-aspected. But, when reversed, this card warns against extravagance and unwise or hasty spending.

The Page of Pentacles
Refers to a young person of either sex, although most probably male, who will act as the bearer of pleasant tidings. This card also signifies the thoughts of someone who hopes to profit by the querent in some way and, when reversed, can signify that the news received could relate to a money loss or an outstanding debt which must be paid at once.

The Page of Swords
This Page also refers to youngsters, probably male, and to feelings of

hostility or dislike. It signifies evil tidings or impediments and, if the querent's question relates to love, could indicate that he has an active rival. If this card falls reversed, it denotes that the querent will discover that someone he trusted as a friend has become a secret enemy and the rival in the matter closest to his heart, whatever this may be.

The best of spreads can be marred by the appearence of the Page of Swords. It is a decisive factor in the querent's affairs because secret rivalry or enmity is impossible to cope with so long as it does remain secret: it is rather like trying to fight a mist.

The exact meanings of the Pages in a divinatory spread depend a great deal on the surrounding cards and should be used to qualify the indications given by these. So, as can be understood, the Pages can be confusing cards in a spread, which is why I suggested leaving them out of the shuffle unless they relate directly to the question raised by the querent.

However, the Pages had quite a different role assigned to them in the ancient mysteries for they also represent the four phases of the Moon in the following order: Page of Cups, New Moon; Page of Wands, First Quarter; Page of Pentacles, Full Moon; and Page of Swords, Last Quarter. They were used as a kind of simple calendar for guidance on when it was best or least auspicious to deal with certain matters.

For instance, lovers' meetings should never be arranged on the day of a New Moon because the Moon is then too near the Sun for it to be fortunate for the woman and deceit could, therefore, spoil the romance before the next New Moon. Similarly, it is not advisable to concern oneself with important commercial issues on the day of the First Quarter, or with financial matters on the actual day of the Full Moon. Nor should one have dealings with rivals or opponents on the day of the Last Quarter or, according to ancient lore, it will be regretted.

One of the things I most like about ancient Egyptian philosophy is that their simple system of psychology, expressed as gods, spirits and powers allied to natural phenomena such as the phases of the Moon, offers such a good insight into human behaviour that it is just as valid today as it was when practised in Egypt thousands of years ago.

The Knights

The Knights of the Tarot have different meanings according to the lay-out of the spread and the gender of the enquirer. For a woman, they can signify men coming into her life, whether as admirers, friends or work associates, as well as the intentions of those she already knows. For a man, they represent male associates and, to a certain extent, his own responses to mental or physical stimulation.

Emotionally, for either sex, the Knights can represent the warring factors in an individual's mind, according to how some member of the male sex impresses him or her. Before further clarification, however, we will examine what the Knights signify in a spread.

The Knight of Cups
To a woman, the Knight of Cups denotes a lover or his thoughts; alternatively, good-will or attention from a man who is a potential admirer. For a man, then, this card signifies his romantic thoughts and feelings, probably towards one particular person. This Knight is a romantic figure, he is imaginative, open-minded and warm-hearted; he is convincing and easily convinced.

The Knight of Pentacles
This Knight stands for a new male friend, unknown to the enquirer at the time of the reading, and the possibility of indiscreet behaviour. Such a man is a charmer who lavishes attention and luxuries on a woman until she falls under his spell, whereupon he gets on this horse and rides away (or even into his sports car!). Men should not trust this slippery character either, for he is likely to lead them astray – and get away with it – especially in business deals.

The Knight of Wands

Signifies a helpful, young man (or one who is younger than the enquirer) who is reliable and conscientious; he has sound business sense and can offer good financial advice. This card also symbolises the helpful thoughts and goodwill of a male friend; if the querent is a male, it can signify his own prudence and helpfulness; and, in a woman's spread, this Knight represents the potential friend, lover and husband she seeks.

The Knight of Swords

If this Knight turns up in a spread, whether or not it is reversed, it warns of a treacherous man – not old, but not very young either – who has wormed his way into the querent's good graces but is certainly not to be trusted. This person will cause quarrels and all sorts of mischief among the enquirer's associates and is a very underhand character. This card also refers to treacherous thoughts.

The Knights of the Minor Arcana have simple predictive meanings, but they can also offer a valuable occult lesson when considered from a philosophical point of view. They can be regarded mainly as the thoughts of men, especially those men who are represented by the Kings in a Tarot spread. For instance, if the man symbolised by the King of Cups has the enquirer in his thoughts, then the Knight of

Cups would lie close to the significator (the card representing the enquirer) in the spread.

Carrying this a stage further, any Knight may also represent some thought form of the enquirer's concerning a particular male; one so powerful that it results in action. So, we will now consider certain other aspects of these cards.

When reversed, the *Knight of Cups* represents underhand dealings; this may refer to the enquirer's own actions or to those of the person who is signified by this card in the spread.

The *Knight of Wands*, when reversed, is a strong warning of danger through the mishandling or poor management of financial affairs, either by the querent or a male who is acting on the enquirer's behalf.

If all *four Knights* turn up together in any one lay-out, this is a sure indication of a future gathering that will lead to strife. This may refer to a party where some of the guests prove inimical to each other or to a contentious business meeting. It can also signify an emotional cross-roads, where the four bold Knights stand for a situation that has become inharmonious on the physical, mental, spiritual and material planes.

In such a situation, follow your heart in the matter. If the Knight of Cups falls on a good card this signifies the best way out of your emotional dilemma. But, if the Knight of Pentacles is the more strongly placed, it portends a destructive infatuation for a female querent and a formidable rival for a male. Should the Knight of Wands be the more strongly placed, prudence is then advised, especially in financial matters. And, when the Knight of Swords is the strongest of the four, it presages trouble and strife.

If accompanied by or laid upon more helpful cards, the worst aspects of the four Knights together in a spread are mitigated but, if placed on or with other cards of evil portent, they warn that disaster will follow if the querent continues with present plans. The cross-roads has been reached, but none of the paths can be recommended with safety because a bold, warring Knight stands on each, barring the way.

The Queens

The four Queens of the Minor Arcana are usually regarded as representing four types of womanhood and their significance in a divinatory spread is therefore simple to understand.

The Queen of Cups

This Queen is any beloved woman. In a spread, she can symbolise the sweetheart, wife or lover in a man's life, or the dearly-loved and faithful friend of a female querent. Whenever this card falls upright, it signifies that the woman represented by the card will help the enquirer's development, emotionally and psychically, by bringing out that person's finer qualities through their shared experiences.

In her most positive aspect, this Queen corresponds to the Madonna, to creativity and intuition, and has a helpful and uplifting influence on the querent's life. But, in her negative role, she symbolises bigotry and the frustration of creativity and may lead the enquirer to regret the relationship if this card falls reversed in a spread.

Her element is Water, thus she is associated with the Water signs: Pisces, Cancer and Scorpio. In the Egyptian pantheon she was linked to Hathor, being credited with the ability to help all love affairs and having a harmonising influence.

The Queen of Pentacles

Represents a wealthy woman who leads a somewhat retiring life and may refer to anyone who fulfils this description and has an encouraging influence on the enquirer. She also signifies the urge to make money or, when this card falls reversed in a spread, difficult financial affairs.

In divination, this Queen often refers to the querent's mother (she may not be financially rich but possesses a wealth of experience) and corresponds to Eve and to the maternal principle. In her positive aspect, she is loving and protective, but in her negative, is possessive and devouring of her young, the kind of woman who will not let her children lead their own lives and prevents them from learning from life's experiences due to her over-protectiveness.

Her element is Earth and she is therefore associated with the Earth signs: Capricorn, Taurus and Virgo. This Queen is credited with the power to grant material wishes and is thus a powerful influence on the querent's life.

The Queen of Wands

This Queen is usually depicted as a prudent, level-headed woman, probably a wife and mother. She has a great and powerful influence on the lives of others and can represent the querent's ideals. With the qualities of a teacher, she signifies wisdom and acts as a spiritual guide, being the source of real strength and knowledge.

This Queen corresponds to Sophia, the woman of ideas, inspiration, mental uplift and spiritual growth, so is a good omen if appearing upright in a spread. Her negative aspect, however, is the negation of all these qualities and when this card is reversed in a spread, therefore, it signifies suspicion, jealousy and mistrust.

Her element is Fire and she is associated with the Fire signs: Aries, Leo and Sagittarius. Her influence is uplifting, success-making and never demanding; her function is to develop the mental and spiritual qualities in others for she brings out their hidden talents and encourages their development.

The Queen of Swords

Usually dubbed as the villainess of the piece for, traditionally, she is supposed to represent an evil-natured woman, or at least to have an unfortunate influence on the enquirer's affairs. She is certainly a fateful woman and a very strong personality.

This Queen corresponds to Helen of Troy, the fatal lover, and is one concept of Eros, god of love. At her best, she is a loving but clinging vine for she is determined to keep that which she considers is her own. At her worst, she is the kind of woman who wrecks lives through her compulsive romantic attachments and, should this card fall reversed in a spread, it signifies scandal, loneliness and unhappiness.

Her element is Air and she is associated with the Air signs: Aquarius, Gemini and Libra. As the magical art is also known as the art of Air, she is a very powerful Queen indeed. Air is a powerful natural force, excellent in moderation, but devastating in excess: whirlwinds, tornadoes and gales. And so it is with this Queen, for she has a dual nature and is a very powerful force. She can be both siren and vampire, she is never the friend of her own sex and hides her ardent, deceitful and selfish nature beneath the guise of powerful love (for a male querent) or devoted (but utterly false) friendship when dealing with another woman.

Thus the four Minor Arcana Queens represent the four types of women who will have opportunities to exert their influence at some time in our lives. Their influences bring various reactions and experiences which can help or hinder the development of our own personalities.

The Kings

The four Tarot Kings of Pentacles, Swords, Wands and Cups correspond to the powers of the four elements of Earth, Air, Fire and Water, respectively. They signify powerful forces yet, in a divinatory spread, have little meaning for they denote strong influences rather than events. So, we will first deal with the predictive meanings of these cards before considering their deeper significance.

Roi de Deniers

The King of Pentacles
Represents a wealthy, influential man who may or may not have friendly feelings towards the enquirer, depending on whether this card

falls upright or reversed in a spread. This figure denotes a worldly-wise, practical person, perhaps a successful businessman who is in a position to advance or inhibit the querent's career. But, when reversed, this card signifies a corrupt, miserly man who is intent only on achieving his own ends.

The King of Swords
This King is a very strong, forceful character whose power may lie either on the worldly, mental, or occult plane. This power may be wielded for or against the querent, depending on whether this card falls upright or reversed. If the latter, it warns the querent that such a powerful person is about to bring a malign influence to bear on his or her life and, therefore, immediate steps must be taken to protect his interests in whichever area of life seems most threatened.

The Kings of Wands
Represents a friendly, sympathetic, family man who will help the enquirer in his or her business affairs if this card falls upright in a spread. When reversed, however, it signifies that such an association will have an ill-effect on the enquirer's business interests. It should therefore be regarded as a warning of danger to any plans or enterprise the querent has in mind at the time of the reading.

The King of Cups

This King represents a warm-hearted, responsible and authoritive figure. He is probably a bachelor and may be a man of science, the Law or the Church. When this card falls upright, it signifies that such a man is well-disposed towards the querent and has his or her interest at heart; when reversed, it denotes that this person will act in an advisory capacity, probably in one of the functions already mentioned, for it also signifies a legal matter that will be resolved satisfactorily.

So much for the exoteric, or outer meanings of these four cards; we will now consider their inner, occult meanings. The four Kings represent material forces, in which all other forces are implied. They also encompass the four quarters of the globe and are the Kings of the Watchtowers who rule the North, South, East and West, as depicted by the Wheel of Ezekiel. The pictograph of this Wheel is also sometimes referred to as the Egyptian Circle or the Gipsy Circle, but both are misnomers because it is actually a symbolic representation of the powers of Earth, Air, Fire and Water and the presiding kings or, more accurately perhaps, resident priests.

It must be remembered that the study of occult forces and powers was divided into four separate Arcana or secret temples of the mysteries. Applicants for the priestly robes were instructed in one of these Arcana up to adept grade; each then had the opportunity to study the others in turn but had to start in each one at the beginning again as an acolyte.

Since the study, practice, use and teaching of only one of the Watchtowers could consume a whole lifetime, it was rare indeed for any priest to embark on the study of all four. This is easy to understand if we bear in mind that the knowledge and study of just one Watchtower, that of Earth for example, gave the adept priest complete power over everything that was on, in or under the Earth. So, few of them reached the summit of their chosen Watchtower because the human life-span is so short.

Yet it is from and by these studies that the great teachers and masters of the world arose – the great magi of history, such as the Buddha and the Christ, the latter being born into the master state. The Bible itself abounds in references to the Watchtowers of wisdom and power; the Scriptures did not mean that they were just places where soldiers watched for the enemy in their terriroty. 'To stand on the watchtower' implied occult awareness, as any student of the Enochian mysteries will know.

So, I hope I have made it plain that a pack of Tarot cards is not just a fortune-telling medium but a book of hidden secrets and wisdom: it is the Book of Thoth in pictorial form. One constantly reads that the mysteries of the Book of Thoth have been lost for ever, but the writers of such statements are mistaken: knowledge can never be lost. It may be scattered, it may not be accessible to those who are only mildly curious, but it cannot cease to exist – if not on this plane, then on a higher one – fragments of that knowledge are contained in the Tarot for those who are determined enough and sincere enough to seek it.

Thoth was not only the Recorder in the Egyptian pantheon, he was also the Keeper of the astral Halls of Records, in which everything ever known was stored after being imprinted on the Astral Light.

CHAPTER 4
The Major Arcana

No. 0 or 22 – The Fool

The Fool's place in the Major Arcana of the Tarot comes at the beginning, as No. 0, or at the end, No. 22; and in some packs this card bears no number at all. As No. 0, the card represents man as he is born, knowing nothing, with all yet to learn, and capable of every mistake and folly that he can make in life. As No. 22, it represents the person at the end of life, when experience has, or should have, taught him wisdom.

One arcanum of this card, then, is that through folly shall man learn wisdom or, in other words, those who do not make mistakes have nothing from which to learn. So, as a general rule, this card should be regarded as a warning of folly or heedlessness if it turns up in a divinatory spread. It represents reckless or unreasonable thoughts and actions which can give rise to unhappiness and upheavals in the querent's circumstances. If the Fool falls in a reversed position, then so much the worse because it signifies that the enquirer is probably following a totally misguided course of action or labouring under an illusion.

This card usually depicts a young man dressed in multi-coloured garments, carrying a small bundle on a stick over one shoulder and, with his eyes upon the skies, about to step over a precipice. He is striding ahead in a careless manner, paying no attention to the small dog at his heels which seems to be trying to bring him down to earth and warn him of the danger that lies immediately ahead.

At a mundane level, the Fool signifies someone who has chosen the wrong turning and goes blithely on his way in search of an illusory dream, making use neither of the light of reason (the Sun) nor intuition (the dog). Thus he is not looking where he is going; he is taking life too lightly or trusting too much to providence. Although it is certainly not wrong to trust in providence, it is fatal to abuse that trust by taking the attitude that something is bound to turn up, without any effort on our part.

Most of us are guilty, at some time or another, of being unreasonable, short-sighted or blithely trotting along as if wearing blinkers, so we are all of us fools to that extent. But as soon as we have the desire to know, to question where we are going and why, then we become less foolish and the path of wisdom starts opening up before us.

Some people remain foolish all their lives, though. These are the ones who are incapable of learning from experience, who are dangerous to themselves and others. No one is quite so dangerous as a fool, for nobody can calculate what a fool is going to do. One can lock up one's goods from a thief or disbelieve a liar, but there is no way whatever of dealing with a fool.

The teaching of every religion admits that mankind will err and make mistakes; each of them teaches that this is how we learn. But they also teach that when a problem is greater than our minds can cope with, we should let the supreme power – whatever we choose to label it – deal with it for us by an act of prayer or faith. Simple as this is, it is yet one of the hardest things we have to learn, perhaps because it is so simple. But over-complication is the hallmark of the fool.

A fool is either one who, knowing better, behaves foolishly, or one who knows nothing at all; and it is far better to be the latter for, knowing nothing, there is everything to learn. Once we admit we know nothing and wish to be taught, we have taken the first step on the path of wisdom. Each Tarot card represents a step on the occult way; each represents an initiation in the soul-life of the searcher after truth.

So, at an occult level, the Fool represents both the grade 0 initiate who knows nothing but wishes to learn and the adept, grade 22. As the latter, it represents the Magus, the person who has learned as much as he is capable of learning in this life and, having achieved the ultimate in knowledge (for him), must then admit that there is so much more to be learned that, in comparison, he knows nothing at all! Thus the adept is not someone who knows everything but one who has learned suffi-cient in this life of the lesson he was sent to learn to realise how little he knows.

Thus the adept becomes as a child again, awed by his own ignorance, and deprecates what little he knows. Just as the study of science does not deny the existence of that which is divine, but in time teaches the scientist how much lies outside man's powers, so does the pursuit of occult knowledge and wisdom teach the adept eventually that compared to God (or the gods) he is a fool. Knowing nothing is childish, but knowing you know nothing is the beginning of wisdom.

From Fool to Magician and back again, that is the occult path. The Major Arcana forms a circle, which has neither beginning nor end, hence the alternative placing of the Fool. Its purpose is to teach us that we are both individuals and an integral part of the whole; that what happens to us has its corresponding echo in the universe, and vice versa. It is a sobering thought – and an important lesson.

So, let us look once again at the card called the Fool and see if it has another message, a deeper meaning, for the one who is starting out on his initiatory journey.

A human being dressed in Fool's motley (symbolising his spiritual condition of knowing nothing or misapplying that which he knows) is blithely stepping out over a precipice with his face turned to the Sun. Some packs also show a crocodile with gaping jaws, waiting for the Fool to step over the edge into his open mouth. At the Fool's heels is a small dog which is trying to attract his attention and pull him back from the edge of the abyss.

Each of us who does not realise that this universe is run by a series of simple but just laws is that Fool with the small bundle of possessions (the sum total of all his past experiences, which amount to very little) slung over his shoulder. The dog represents one of the aspects of the Moon – intuition – which can act as a warning if only it is heeded in time. The crocodile symbolises an ancient Egyptian deity, Sebek, the dark, destroying god of mental and physical destruction. The Sun represents providence but, as the Fool is failing to see what is at his feet, as he is failing to use the wits and sense that the creator granted him, he is a Fool indeed, for he has everything yet to learn.

Yet, if he learns the lessons that are his to learn, if he casts out fear (the crocodile) and ignorance (the abyss), if he uses his intuition (the dog) and talents (his bundle), then he becomes the Magus, unconcerned with worldly matters, with his eyes and thoughts concentrated on his ultimate aim (the Sun), that which is divine, and thus walks confidently towards his goal with wisdom not folly at his heels.

No. 1 – The Magician

The first card of the Tarot trumps, the Magician, signifies the power of true magic, the ability to cause and influence events. This card is a symbol of that power which we all have within us because it is as much part of man as is his own bloodstream. So, the only difference between the strong person who can influence events at will and the one who becomes the helpless victim of circumstances is a matter of training in the use of occult power.

THE MAGICIAN

That power is thought, no more and no less, which is why the appearance of the Magician in a divinatory spread refers to the querent's state of mind. If the card fall upright, it denotes that all is well, the enquirer's mind is ready to accept the lessons necessary to learn how to use and control the mind's force. When reversed, however, it shows that his or her mind is in turmoil and he is not seeing his problems in their true perspective.

Thought is the most powerful factor in life and is the essence of the occult. Out thoughts reflect the sort of people we are and dictate those we will become; everything has its origins in thought. Emotions and feelings follow thought, with good or ill effects according to whether the thought that preceded such feelings was constructive or destructive.

The part of your being that corresponds to the Magician of the Tarot is, therefore, your mentality and, according to your ability or inability to use this properly, you can attain to either great occult powers or none at all. In order to develop your magic powers, you must learn to think clearly, to divorce your thoughts from your emotions initially and to realise that thought is a great, though invisible power.

Note that the words 'occult powers' are used to describe actual magical forces set in motion by the use of clear, trained thought. Psychic powers are different, they arise through feelings or from those 'sensitives' who respond to the thoughts and feelings of others, who can pick up or tune in to external conditions. The practising magician, however, is not so concerned with picking up or translating the feelings of others as he is with causing the right conditions to occur.

So, if you want to know how to develop your latent occult (as opposed to psychic) abilities, you must first learn how to think clearly; which is not as easy as it sounds. Very few people can think clearly because this means that they must be able to listen to all points of view and to reason which one holds the maximum truth.

Clear thinking, therefore, requires the power of analysis – cold judgement divorced from feeling. It is necessary to be able to separate reasoning powers from emotions, to divide the physical from the mental, because emotions have their source in the body, whereas intellect is of the mind alone. When one has learned to think clearly and to analyse one's findings, the next step is to think constructively, to apply one's reasoning powers to the problem under consideration.

If we can think clearly, we can act in a simple, straightforward manner; but if our minds are confused, our words and actions become confused, too, and we aggravate our problems. So we have to train our minds to deal with our problems and, once we apply our intellects, we usually find that most of our troubles are due to our own actions.

Perhaps we have not used the correct methods in the first place, have not made sufficient efforts or have allowed others to form opinions and do our thinking for us; thus we make mistakes and create problems for ourselves. Yet mistakes are there for us to learn from.

That is why it can sometimes be wrong to try and hold back friends and loved ones from certain experiences; they may need such experiences for their own edification. So concentrate on your own problems, decide whether they have arisen through your own errors because, if so, you are the only one who can solve them. And, once you have acknowledged these points, the Magician within will offer help.

All knowledge – and therefore all power – is there to be found by those who seek it, but it is granted in exact proportion to the seeker's understanding. In other words, magical powers are not given until the mind of the student is sufficiently widened to accept them. Each of us has different lessons to learn in this life and, therefore, has fortunate and unfortunate times to experience in order to attain this end. Initiation does not take place behind the locked doors of a man-made temple but comes through the trials of life itself, each of which is harder than the one preceding it.

The true magician understands this; he realises the necessity of certain troubles through which we must all pass; he knows that they do not come haphazardly or in vain. This is why the planet Uranus, the Transmuter, has connections with card No. 1 of the Tarot trumps. Uranus has the power to transmute evil into good, so the power wielded by the magician can truly be described as Uranian.

The symbolism depicted on this card describes, in pictorial form, the knowledge required by the would-be magician. The Magician is shown lifting his right hand towards the heavens (the spiritual plane) and with his left pointing down (the material plane), thus indicating the two ways open to students of magical powers.

In front of the figure is a round table or altar, signifying the serpent with its tail in its mouth – wisdom without end. On the altar are the four basic magical weapons or tools – the wand, sword, chalice and platter which, incidentally, correspond to the four suits of the Tarot.

The wand or staff symbolises the conjuring up of magical forces; the sword represents the wielding and directing of that power; the cup or chalice symbolises the physical (the vessel) and spiritual (flowing power) elixir of life; and the platter or plate corresponds to the Ace of Pentacles, signifying spiritual and material riches.

This card, then, depicts the figure and trappings of the ritual magician, representing both the student and the adept – he who has mastered some or all of the occult laws and powers, discovered how to apply them effectively to worldly matters and learned to use them wisely. In acquiring such knowledge ritual plays an important part for it is by its use that the novice, in time, learns to differentiate between black and white magic – perhaps better described as that which has a lasting beneficial effect (white magic) and that which merely secures a temporary advantage (black).

But the novice will soon find that although black magic may seem just as effective as the other kind, it has a hidden snag: the initial success achieved usually leads to sudden and unexpected disaster. A high degree of intelligence is necessary for all ritual magic, so a successful practitioner will be far too intelligent to waste his talents on those things which serve no purpose and have no lasting effect; this is the message of card No. 1, the Magician.

No. 2 – The High Priestess

Number 2 of the Major Arcana, the High Priestess (or, as she is called in some packs, the Female Pope) represents lunar power and, therefore, has strong connexions with Tarot card No. 18, the Moon. She symbolises the New Moon and the feminine creative forces; Isis, the Mother of Wisdom; the influences behind impending change and the ebb and flow of mundane and occult tides.

Some of the positive qualities signified by this card are adeptship in the occult sciences, mysticism, divination and esoteric ritual and practice; which is why the High Priestess often denotes the interpreter of a

Tarot spread. The appearance of this card in a divinatory spread usually presages dramatic changes in the querent's life.

If upright, such changes are likely to be of a beneficial nature and can be expected to take place shortly after the next New Moon following the reading. However, when reversed, the negative aspects of the High Priestess come into play and these are the opposite of those mentioned above. Thus, any impending changes in the enquirer's life are likely to prove unfortunate or misguided.

It is perhaps worth noting at this point the symbolism depicted on this card because it will help to illustrate the arcana behind the second Tarot trump. The High Priestess is shown at the entrance to a temple, seated between the twin pillars of ignorance and enlightenment, one black column and one white, symbolising negative and positive forces.

Draped between these pillars is a veil, in front of which is the female figure, thus the High Priestess is guarding the entrance to the temple from the uninitiated who can only pass through when they have learned her mysteries. On her lap she holds the Tora scroll, the Book of the Law, signifying that she possesses arcane wisdom and secret knowledge of nature and the universe.

On her breast is a solar cross or, in some packs, an Egyptian ansated one, and at her feet is a crescent Moon, indicating the powerful lunar forces associated with this card. The High Priestess wears the head-dress of Isis, the Sun's disc supported by the horns of the Moon, representing its New and Last Quarters.

It therefore becomes clear from the symbolism that this card represents powerful forces. The High Priestess is the female interpreter of arcane law, the Mother of Wisdom, and is able to operate the magic creative force through the use of imagination and will; she is, in fact, the personification of true lunar power. Not herself a goddess, she is the High Priestess of the Temple of Isis.

Thus she served Isis, perhaps the most beloved of all the ancient Egyptian deities, who was regarded as Mother of the Skies and of Wisdom and, therefore, represented the power of the Moon itself. And, according to the state of wisdom she herself had attained, the High Priestess was the interpreter or channel for this power and, as such, was an oracle who could be consulted not only about personal matters but about anything at all because she was handmaiden to Isis, Goddess of Wisdom Incarnate.

The High Priestess of the Temple of Isis, the House of the Moon, wielded enormous power in Egypt and no political or philosophical changes could be made without her consent for she epitomised the feminine mysteries. She understood lunar forces and applied them to daily life. In much the same way that the Moon controls the sea's tides, her priestess controlled the affairs of men. Credited with the ability to know when something must wane or pass away, she had the influence to dictate its passing.

The Egyptian goddess Isis wore another aspect, that of Hathor, the Sacred Cow (hence the Moon's horns on the High Priestess's head-dress). In her Hathor form, the goddess represented all that was good in the ordinary, human woman – the mother, the bearer of burdens, the nourisher and man's helpmate. Thus the Moon embodied all the feminine principles and was given rulership over all of them. But, just as the goddesses of the Moon symbolise different aspects, so do the Moon's phases; and Tarot trump No. 2 is concerned with the New Moon.

The New Moon marks the beginning of a new cycle and is, therefore, that lunar aspect which relates to creative thought – to imagination, inspiration and innovation. It also refers to the spiritually awakened individual who is able to distinguish between imagination and illusion, inspiration and delusion – someone who has learned to control imagination and does not allow it to control him.

This last point is important as learning the correct use of imagination is essential for this is what gives birth to ideas – the creation of thought itself. Someone who lacks this control is like the female adept of the Temple of Isis who misuses her powers and becomes a servant instead of the mistress of occult forces; thus her qualities degenerate.

Change becomes inconstancy because she can no longer control the ebb and flow of the astral sea and, like flotsam, is tossed by uncontrol-led forces; the landscape of her mind is shadowed by mists of illusion instead of being illuminated by the serene light of the Moon. This, then, is the negative aspect of the second Tarot trump.

The enquirer should regard it as a warning if this card falls reversed in a spread for it signifies that although the forthcoming changes in his or her circumstances (which particular aspect of life will be affected is indicated by this card's position in a spread) may seem fortunate initially, such improvements may prove to be illusory or transient.

Certainly changes are presaged by the appearance of the High Priestess in a spread because this card is Moon ruled and, just as this orb waxes and wanes, so too do the affairs of mankind. It is a powerful card and represents strong influences which are bound to have an obvious effect upon the enquirer's life, for good or ill according to other factors and, most significantly, according to his level of enlightenment.

For, above all else, the second Tarot trump denotes spiritual awareness, inner illumination; that deeper understanding that cannot be conveyed by mere words. The High Priestess sits at the very threshold of the temple; she guards the gateway to the higher mysteries and exemplifies all the characteristics of one skilled in the occult arts.

She has obtained her exalted position through rigid training, study and practise; she signifies not only the natural power which you have within you but also the degree of power to which you can attain. The High Priestess is at the summit of her calling and has learned to control the forces of nature, to balance mental and physical, positive and negative; she is intuitive and perceptive; she possesses knowledge and wisdom; and is mistress of all she surveys.

No. 3 – The Empress

Number 3 of the Tarot, the Empress, signifies the female principle and embodies both the higher and lower aspects of Venus, her planetary ruler. She represents Gaea, the Earth, and is the fecund mother of all that grows; she is, in fact, Mother Nature and Queen of Life.

The Empress has sovereignty over the spiritual, creative forces and is shown seated upon a kind of throne, holding a sceptre in her right hand and wearing a diadem studded with jewels on her head. These symbols denote her queenly status and the jewels represent stars, signifying her links with the skies and the open air. To her right is a shield (which is depicted as heart-shaped in some Tarot packs) bearing the astrological symbol for Venus which is, of course, also the crux ansata or ankh, Egyptian symbol of life.

In the foreground, at the Empress's feet, is a field of wheat and in the background is a fertile landscape, both of which symbolise her rulership over nature and of everything that grows. Water can be glimpsed between the trees and this represents the Water of Life, the vivifying principle. Clearly, then, this card signifies the generative forces, fertility and productivity: it is, in fact, the essence of fecundity.

When used for divinatory purposes, the Empress card stands for happily married bliss or a joyous betrothal as well as for a love affair. So, when this card falls upright in a spread, it signifies the triumph of true love but, if reversed, it signals the end of a love affair. It is as well to remember, too, that although the Empress represents a happy, fulfilled woman, this term can be applied equally well to a woman with a career as to a wife or mother because one can be emotionally involved with an aim or ambition as well as with people.

Also, as the Empress relates to the harvest Moon, her appearance in a spread may presage a birth, either literally or figuratively. She can, for instance, indicate the birth of an idea because the Empress signifies creativity and imagination. Equally, she may denote that the enquirer is due to reap the harvest of past efforts and will soon be rewarded with a material gain of some kind.

It is important to remember that the Tarot trumps are symbolic cards and should not be taken simply at face value when interpreting a divinatory spread. They stand for the forces behind present and future events, so their meanings may not be immediately obvious and they should, therefore, be read in the light of the enquirer's personal circumstances.

On the mundane level, the positive attributes of the Empress are domestic happiness, warmth and comfort, initiative and the aims of life itself; her negative aspects are disharmony, dissolution, dissipation and waste of material resources, also instability. In contrast to the High Priestess, who is primarily concerned with spiritual matters, the Empress relates more to physical and emotional concerns, for her fundamental principle is the conservation and development of life itself.

Esoterically, however, the Empress has a much higher meaning and her arcane title is Daughter of the Mighty Ones. These mystical beings inhabited the spaces between the stars and their task was to ensure that no one interfered with the rhythm of the universe. Known also as the Watchers, their duty was to keep the planets on their courses and to uphold the universal laws. They kept watch from the four watchtowers and, aided by their Daughter, countered any disturbance by the administration of the appropriate element.

Hence, if lunar forces were upset, these were counterbalanced by water, the Moon's element. Perhaps this example helps to explain the occult causes of floods, for the Watchers' retaliatory measures could, quite fairly, be described as an excess of waters, or a flood. Of course, such disturbances were on an occult plane but, should the same principle apply on a more mundane level, one dreads to think what the likely effects would be should mankind's aggressive actions upset the vibrations of the peaceful orb we call the Moon!

So, in her role as Daughter, the Empress helped to balance the forces of nature if these were disturbed through man's intrepidity, impudence or ignorance. This aspect of the Empress is not so dissimilar from her guise in the Tarot for here, too, she is credited with power over the laws of nature and, being Venus-ruled, is a 'balancing' or harmonising influence.

In her Venusian aspect, the Empress also represents the seas and pools in which life itself originated; and the sigil used as the astrological sign for Venus (emblazoned on the Empress's shield) combines both the male and female principle. Thus the waters were the mother of all life – the watery womb from which all living creatures sprang – and Venus, the goddess of mythology, was sea-born, she arose from the waters and her beginning, therefore, echoed that of mankind.

Venus, of course, is also the goddess of love and the third Tarot trump is a love card. Like her male counterpart, the Emperor (No. 4 of the Major Arcana), the Empress is a mature person. She is no longer the young, untutored maiden she once was, but has become a wife and mother, having been engulfed in love of another. She is the mundane representation of a happily married woman who has found her true mate and affinity.

Hers is the compassionate, all-encompassing love of Venus, the gentle planet, not the ardent passion of mere physical or sexual attraction. It is, in fact, true love; understanding. To understand someone is to know all there is to know about that person, to see them with the eyes of truth and not through rose-tinted spectacles; and to know all is to forgive all, for knowledge means the wisdom to accept facts.

Real love is undemanding, it is unselfish, and its benefits endure because it is a creative, not a destructive force. Passions are quickly spent but genuine love develops slowly, it grows stronger with the passing of time and unites the two halves until they become one.

Out of such mutual understanding will come a harvest of good, lasting things. This can mean happiness on the mundane plane, since the slings and arrows of fortune cannot penetrate the shield of mutual love and trust. Love means far more than two people caught in the grip of a strong emotion. It incorporates destiny itself, the occult laws, and the powers and principalities that govern the affairs, life and fate of the world itself.

The Empress and her arcana are strongly associated with Venus in her many aspects, thus she symbolises human love (Venus in Taurus) but also divine love (Venus in Libra) and personifies the creative, unifying forces of nature on a universal scale. So, this is basically a bountiful card, signifying all the good things of life, and can, therefore, presage material or financial benefits as well as emotional comfort and security.

No. 4 – The Emperor

The fourth card of the Major Arcana is the personification of the male principle – the Emperor. This figure represents temporal power – kingship, leadership and government of the material world. He is a dominant, authoritative character and has strong associations with the planet Mars and its metal, iron, signifying will.

The symbolism of this trump illustrates these points graphically. In most packs, the Emperor is depicted as a mature male figure (signifying endurance) seated on a throne (denoting temporal power) decorated with rams' heads (Aries, the symbol for Mars). In his right hand is a sceptre (male potency) topped by an orb (representing the world) surmounted by a solar cross or ankh (enduring life and generative energy); and at his left side is a shield blazoned with an eagle (another symbol of virility).

In a Tarot spread, this card therefore represents the male attributes of authority, strength, courage and will-power; and, when upright, denotes a successful man. The reversed card stands for the spiritual or softer elements of the Emperor's nature, including benevolence, clemency, understanding and pity; and can signify a man in a quandary. In a divinatory spread, the Emperor card usually signifies the querent himself or, if the reading is for a woman, the male interest in her life.

As with all the Tarot trumps, there are deeper meanings in this card. At one level, the Emperor denotes man's finest attributes, wisdom and power, whereas, at a lower level, it represents a man who exercises dominion over his own life, possessions and inner nature. So the message of card No. 4 is that any man can become an Emperor of Wisdom and have dominion over his chosen sphere.

In the old mystery schools, any man who had followed occult teaching and learned to apply its wisdom benefited others and himself and, therefore, had attained a fair share of good fortune and success. As soon as any aspirant for occult honours achieved knowledge, power, worldly standing and the material benefits that accompany these attributes, he became an occult emperor.

But sovereigns only continue to reign through continual watchfulness, so the occult student had to learn to remain watchful, to heed the warning voice that cautioned him that he was on dangerous ground or about to commit a folly. He had to learn how to maintain his material progress through inner strength, the ability to be firm with his own weaknesses, and thus combat potential enemies of his moral and spiritual fibre.

A successful ruler needs to be brave, true, loyal and steadfast because only then can he hope to rule himself and others with authority and impunity. So it behoved him to be stern with his weaknesses, which are those of his ruling planet Mars – foolhardiness, selfishness, susceptibility, aggressiveness and unbridled passion, the desire to possess, dominate and be admired.

Mars is a forceful planet and, when its powers are properly used, can make a man an emperor but, if misused, can make him destroy himself. This planet rules the vital life-force – Kundalini, the serpent-fire – and all occultists know the danger of unleashing its power deliberately without also imposing the iron control of will. When Kundalini becomes unbalanced, which it can do accidentally, the result is often one of those destructive, obsessive infatuations that upset both mind and body because this powerful force is strongly associated with the more physical aspects of love.

Infatuation is a physical and mental obsession that is temporarily stronger than true, enduring love – the gentle, self-sacrificing love of Venus. It can override reason and, under its spell, people can destroy their marriages, their homes and even their careers by causing pain to their nearest and dearest through their selfish actions and, sometimes, actual cruelty. Reason gives way to entirely emotional judgements, with the object of the suffer's infatuation receiving all the attention while others enjoy no consideration at all.

Fortunately, however, the transits of the fiery planet Mars are of short duration, so infatuation is soon over, its influence is only temporary. Yet whether or not the victim of this potentially destructive force can rebuild his life after passion is spent will depend not only on the love, patience and understanding of others but also on his inner resources – his strength of character, his ability to control the kundalini force.

For, in order to master mankind and reign over them, the individual must first master himself. Before progress can be made he has to learn what kind of person he is, he has to face his inner self, develop the strength necessary to conquer his faults and control his weaknesses because only then can he hope to resist temptation, to meet and overcome challenges. This is the arcane meaning behind card No. 4 – challenge.

There are times in life when good fortune seems to come from issuing a challenge to fate, or one's adversaries, and in some Tarot packs the Emperor card actually shows the male figure holding a sword in his left hand, thus underlining the Martian attributes associated with this card.

Nowadays, of course, we cannot summon our enemies to mortal combat with bugle blast but must fight with modern weapons such as letters, telephone calls and personal interviews. Nevertheless, if you have a problem to tackle, it is your fighting spirit that will carry you through to victory.

Thus it is obvious that this card has a reference to troubles which cannot be ignored but have to be dealt with as though they were real-life adversaries. Its appearance in a spread can, therefore, advise the querent that his difficulties must be brought out into the open and tackled, no matter what the nature of his problem may be. In other words, in this context, the Emperor signifies that most troubles have a concrete foundation.

Often, a problem will expand to alarming proportions because of the human failing of hoping that something or someone will turn up and settle it for us. The worst offenders are those people who have very little to contend with in life, who have been so buffered against its stark realities that when trouble does arise they flounder about helplessly. They have not learned that life is a challenge, that its good things have to be earned and are not theirs simply for the asking.

Yet life is a school, not just a long holiday, and inside each of us is a challenger, the Emperor, crying out for something to fight and win, something that will add to our mental and moral fibre. The emperor within can make a boy a man, even a superman; it can also give a woman the mental and moral strength to overcome adversity: it is the hidden desire within all of us to meet and overcome every challenge.

No. 5 – The High Priest

Number 5 in the Tarot trumps, the High Priest, Pope or Hierophant (according to which Tarot pack is used) represents power, inspiration, intelligence and discrimination. When reversed in a divinatory spread, it signifies the opposite qualities, either in others or in the enquirer.

When this card appears in a spread it is usually because the querent has forgotten, or will not acknowledge that there are powers beyond those of mankind and that they have not been properly appealed to for help in his dilemma. It is not enough just to pray, one must pray constructively and, even then, prayers may not be enough without the faith that they can be answered. This, above all, is the meaning of No. 5 of the Major Arcana.

All of us have trials and tribulations to face at one time or another in our lives, some of which may seem too immense for our strength to overcome. It is times like these when our subconscious minds — our secret voices – can be of help: can be our inspiration. This is another aspect of the High Priest, for he represents inspiration, not the same kind of inspiration as that signified by the Moon, but divine inspiration – the inner voice.

Everyone who reads these words and has a problem can make an experiment which will prove that the secret voice within is a reality and not mere myth. Devote the night hours to meditating upon your problem and pray that you may be told how to solve it; do not pray for your troubles to be removed from your path because they come to teach you something. Ask, instead, that you may be inspired with a solution.

In the morning, some will wake up with the answer clear in their minds; others will later receive a flash of true inspiration which offers the only possible solution. Thus you will have learnt, for all time, the powers of card No. 5 which represents the link between yourself and the creator; it is a true channel of communication and knowledge.

According to ancient Egyptian teachings, the High Priest had attained the Ring of Power and was credited with the ability to perform magic of all kinds. It would seem, therefore, that someone with such powers would need to be saintly indeed not to use magic for his own purposes, not to descend to craftiness and guile on occasions, because then, as now, the priesthood was concerned with temporal as well as spiritual power.

Yet, is it so wrong to use occult powers for oneself? After all, the powers are there to help us; we are here to help one another. How, then, can we relieve the real miseries of others if we ourselves need help? In any case, no one, by magic or occult practice, can get more out of life than they contribute to it.

'There is a hidden priest in most of us', is a common occult maxim, implying that nearly all humans are fascinated by religious mysteries, mystic symbolism and traditional ritual, and would like to know more about such things. This is one of the interpretations of the High Priest of the Tarot: it can represent the questing soul in search of truth.

Not everybody develops 'the priest within', the seeds of occult power that lie within each of us, because very few people are prepared to make sacrifices or have the necessary determination to study the subject fully enough. It takes time and patience to test out occult formulae; it takes courage, too, to learn to accept disasters that have been self-invoked. There is no comfortable, safe road to occult knowledge and no real initiations take place upon the dream plane. Each piece of knowledge is bought with personal sacrifice and pain; each step is marked by the Tower's ordeals.

The true basis of all occult study is a reverent desire to understand that which is divine: to this end the great mystery schools of the past were dedicated. Occultism is no more nor less than the study of religion; of the links between the godhead and mankind. 'As above, so below', is probably the best known occult maxim of all time; and it is the basis of all occult teachings.

It implies and accepts that positive and negative are necessary; that light and darkness are twins, that they are bound together. True occultists do not accept that good and evil are two separate forces; they realise that it is not as simple as that. Good intentions and actions, if misplaced, can have an evil effect. Equally, if someone tries to do you a bad turn, it could turn out to your ultimate benefit because, in the long run, man is not the arbiter.

The study of the occult is, fundamentally, an attempt to understand the workings of the laws of creation; and for the individual to harmonise himself with those laws. Thus, he would become his own priest or hierophant with no need of a mediator. In his studies of the essence of the universe, the occult student finds a link between everything that happens and nature itself.

So, before even the simplest ritual can be undertaken successfully, the occultist must know what can or cannot be done and why, because no magical ritual aimed against the natural law of the universe can hope to succeed. It is this knowledge, in fact, that must come first: it is the primary thing that must be learned before any ritual is attempted. The Hierophant is depicted seated on a throne, the throne of knowledge; but until he has obtained such knowledge, the Ring of Power is not his to use or misuse.

Not that anyone with any real knowledge would dream of setting harmful effects into motion, of course. Such a person would be aware that magic aimed at harming others would be bound to fail. Magic moves in a circle: any power sent out must return to its source – he who sent it. What is more, this force is multiplied, it returns sevenfold, so the magician of ill intent would damage himself far more than the person whom he set out to harm.

Magic is the study of natural laws and their uses, it is not the study of the supernatural. Supernatural means, quite literally, above nature and nothing in this world is above nature, as consideration of the word shows plainly. The dictionary definition of nature is: 'the universe; the essence or essential qualities of a thing; the natural law'. So, anyone who has already grasped the fundamental laws of nature and is prepared to work with them has the ability to perform ritual, to use the magical signs and forces, and has already become a hierophant, or priest of the gods.

The symbols associated with the High Priest are numerous, yet in most packs the figure is depicted with one hand raised in benediction, while the other holds the triple cross, symbolising the power that links the spiritual, intellectual and material worlds. There are usually two posts or pillars shown on this card, one to either side of the seated priest, and these signify the duality already mentioned – the freedom of choice that we all possess.

You, too, can attain the Ring of Power – the full development of the particular occult abilities that are within you. Like the Hermit who searches for truth with the lantern of faith, you must find you own way, but do not be afraid to use occult powers to help yourself; this is not evil, simply sensible.

No. 6 – The Lovers

Number 6 of the Tarot trumps, the Lovers, is often mistakenly regarded as being concerned only with love affairs, mainly due to its title, yet it is not a love card except on a superficial level. In most packs this card shows a young man standing between two females with a celestial being floating above their heads, sometimes identified as Cupid or Eros, about to shoot an arrow from his bow at one of the figures below.

So, on a mundane level, this card can be regarded as depicting a triangular love affair because the male figure is apparently in a state of indecision between the two women and, as such, it often crops up in a Tarot spread before the rupture of a love affair or marriage. Yet this interpretation only expresses the outer meaning of this card which could, perhaps, be more aptly called the Rivals because it signifies those situations in life when a choice must be made.

Such a choice may be between two loves, two modes of conduct or two different ways of life and, in some instances, these may be connected. But this may not necessarily be the case because each Tarot card has many different meanings which must be interpreted according to the personal circumstances of the querent.

So, should this card appear reversed in a spread, it is a warning that the enquirer is in danger of making the wrong decision, of choosing the wrong person, path, or whatever and that trouble will result from this error of judgement, no matter what that decision may refer to. If upright, however, it signifies that the querent has simply reached a decisive point in his or her life and is advised to make a choice carefully, with all due consideration, for it can change the course of his destiny.

In an allegorical sense, the winged being on the Lovers card can represent Eros (Cupid), the god of love, about to awaken his beloved, Psyche, with the touch of his arrow. 'Psyche' is also the Greek word for the soul and the celestial figure could also refer to Hermes (Mercury), the winged messenger of the gods.

Mercury, of course, is associated with the intellect, so this card can symbolise the awakening of the soul, or spiritual awareness. And, as choice or rivalry is implicit in this card, it could be interpreted as denoting a conflict between intellect and intuition, reason and emotion. Thus the deeper meanings of this card begin to emerge.

The Lovers can reveal the reason behind any emotional hesitation, indecision or instability because, when our minds are disturbed by emotions of any kind – whether love, sorrow, fear, hatred or whatever – we are unable to think straight. This is why No. 6 is one of the trumps governed by Thoth in the Egyptain pantheon, Hermes in the Greek, and Mercury in the Roman, each signifying the power of mentality, and is given the zodiacal rulership of Gemini, a dual sign, which also represents emotions versus reason.

Emotions arise from physical causes and, therefore, can and do disturb the mind. Fear can cause someone to be depressed and downcast; love can make that same person feel exalted beyond all reason; and hatred may impel him to act foolishly. Yet emotions, by their very nature, are ephemeral: time can exhaust them or tone them down to manageable proportions. Mentality, on the other hand, is limitless: the more it is used, the greater and more powerful it becomes.

So, in the battle between emotion and reason, the physical versus the mental, we have to learn to strike a balance, to use the wisdom that we have gained through past experience and not to ignore its existence due to the strength of our feelings. We have all, on occasions, done something that we knew we should not do when under the influence of strong emotion. But to continue in such actions when our minds tell us we are doing wrong, or when the situation is hopeless, is to allow our physical-emotional natures to overrule our intellects. This puts us on the level of animals, who act from instinct or desire; this is when we can harm ourselves unless we take time to reason and allow Mercury, the power of the mind, to guide us. For, if we can learn to consider our emotional problems calmly instead of enacting them, they will be halved immediately.

Unfortunately, however, few of us act sensibly and equably when deeply involved and, too often, the calm voice of reason is drowned by the roar of emotion's tide. If we allow such situations to persist unchecked, we are doomed to disaster because the mind and body are indivisable and we must, therefore, learn to balance their opposing influences; this is one of the messages of the sixth Tarot trump, the Lovers.

There is also a deeper, arcane meaning behind this card. It is symbolised by the three human figures which, in this context, signify what are known as the Children of the Voice. The voice is that of the universal creator and the children represent echoes of that voice. In this sense, the trinity depicted on this trump refers not to the Father, Son and Holy Ghost of Christianity but to a far older trinity of the ancient mysteries – Madriax, Peripsol and Gmicalzoma; and the winged being floating above the three is a kerub (not a cherub), a heavenly or celestial being whose arrows represents direct, controlled thought – will – which flies straight as an arrow to its objective.

Putting this symbolism together from its mystic aspect, we find that if offers a pictorial clue to an ancient magical system which involves the rites and ceremonies of the angel Metatron who is strongly associated with this card. Thus those who possess the will to be so may be instructed in the ancient mysteries by the Children of the Voice; they will have their mentalities elevated to such a plane that they can comprehend what they see and hear.

This does not imply that one should or could employ such powerful forces in order to receive 'astral instruction' in the everyday trivialities of man, for one does not need the mighty power of the Children of the Voice for such mundane purposes. And the ability to know for what the mysteries are intended and to use them for their correct purposes is exactly what is entailed in that occult practice which is known as magic.

The initiate must learn early in his studies not to take a sledgehammer to crack a nut – one does not need the supreme invocation to Air simply in order to produce a cupful of wind when it is required.

The mighty forces behind the mystic Tarot are not, and never were used as servants of humanity; for the lesser can never command the greater and that which is superior can never serve.

There are few problems within the range of humanity that cannot be solved by common sense and, where that is lacking, there are always those wiser than ourselves who can help us to understand, to learn how to achieve the balance necessary to overcome the rivalry denoted by card No. 6 and to make the correct choices.

No. 7 – The Chariot

The seventh card of the Tarot's Major Arcana is the Chariot, commonly known as the Chariot of the Sun. Yet, despite its title, this card is lunar-ruled because the Moon, which reflects the Sun's light, is the conveyor or chariot of the Sun. The numbering of this card underlines this fact because seven is a lunar not a solar number.

This number has always been regarded as one of great occult significance. Ancient religions placed the seven days of the week under the rulership of the Moon which, as the carrier of the Sun's light, was responsible for relaying solar emanations to the Earth on each day. Thus each day was credited with specific properties according to the nature of its vibration.

The lunar month is, of course, 28 days or, more accurately, four periods of seven days, each of which relates to one of the Moon's quarters. And, as the Moon is a crescent at her first and last phases, she symbolises a cup, and into that cup are poured the differing vibrations of the seven days. This, though, is just one of the numerous facets of the Chariot's arcana.

Another aspect of the Chariot of the Sun is the relationship between the two deities symbolised by the Sun and Moon in classical mythology. The Sun is regarded as a male orb and was represented by Apollo, God of the Sun, while the Moon, being female, was personified by Artemis, Goddess of the Moon. Both are equally necessary and of equal power and, in conjunction, were regarded as twin deities who could provide divine help.

Such divine help – providence – is a very significant factor of this card's arcana and is why it is regarded as auspicious if the Chariot turns up in a Tarot spread. However, its roots lie in the ancient practice of performing the powerful Sun-Moon ceremonies at those times when these two heavenly bodies were 'in relation', that is working together or occupying their chariot of dual power. These occasions were the Moon's Quarter days when invocations would be made according to the lunar phases.

The New Moon relates to the beginning of a cycle, therefore if help was required for any new venture or for the growth of a project, invocations were made to the New Moon; and some indication of divine intervention, however slight, would be received by the First Quarter if the prayers were sufficiently sincere to warrant a response. The Moon at the Full signifies the chariot in full power, when those things requested or begun at the New Moon come to fulfilment.

The Full Moon thus indicates the culmination of growth and its passing marks the start of the waning period. Full Moon and Last Quarter rituals were, therefore, concerned with the dispelling of unwanted or evil influences and conditions. In the dark of the Moon came a period of rest from magic and prayer because the Moon does not then carry the Sun's light. After this, the whole cycle of invocation and petitioning for divine help began again at the next New Moon.

Thus did the ancients call upon the heavenly powers to help them achieve success in their ventures and these same solar-lunar influences are embodied in card No. 7. It signifies triumph over obstacles, success in any undertaking and the help and protection of providence. Unexpected help should therefore come if it is needed whenever this card appears in a Tarot spread.

Unlike most of the Tarot trumps, the Chariot's appearance is a hopeful omen, whether it falls upright or reversed, except in one or two instances and, even then, it merely indicates the possibility of error rather than portending disastrous circumstances. The Chariot can, therefore, be regarded as a very encouraging card because it promises success.

Being lunar-ruled, this card's promises are fulfilled speedily whenever the Chariot falls upright in a spread. When reversed, such success or victory will not be immediate but will only materialise as a result of continued effort. Yet, to fail at the first, second, or even third attempt means little except that the time is not yet right for whatever endeavour you are engaged in to culminate in success.

It is an occult truth that success (as opposed to a stroke of sheer good fortune or luck) comes only as a result of repeated efforts, a refusal to be discouraged and trial and error in attempting to make one's ambitions come true. But one should not be discouraged by repeated failure because it is equally true that when success comes as a result of application and repeated endeavour, such success will last, for it is the success of experience.

Life itself is the great initiator and the Chariot completes the first septenary of the Major Arcana; thus, on an arcane level, this card marks the culmination of the initiate's first stage of development. To drive the golden Chariot of the Sun needs skill, one can't just jump in and drive away but must learn to drive, and it is in trying and failing that we learn. Then, one day we are ready, the time is ripe, the golden chariot stops for us and we are on our way to the lasting success that follows true and hard effort.

All efforts that are made must be of a mental and physical character, since both are required if there is to be any hope of eventual success. The force of our efforts increases with each successive attempt until it finally reaches sufficient strength to cut through and overcome all obstacles. Then the desired result can be attained, but only when the time is ripe. First, we must acquire the wisdom of experience which signals the end of the first stage of our initiation for, like the charioteer on Tarot card No. 7, we are all master of our own destinies.

Control over our worldly fortunes is symbolised by the crown and sceptre of the male figure depicted on this card, for it is not a kingly or priestly figure but one who has conquered on the lower or earthly plane. He has, therefore, learned to direct the elementary forces for his own ends and the four posts that support the chariot's canopy represent the four elements – Fire, Earth, Air and Water; and the canopy refers to celestial protection.

The two horses (or oxen, or sphinx-headed lions, according to the Tarot pack used) that draw the chariot on its triumphal passage through life denote the opposing forces of positive and negative, good and evil, material and spiritual, for one is black, the other white. So the charioteer, like the initiate on his first journey, must learn to balance the opposing forces of his nature, his personality, which is symbolised by the chariot itself.

So each of us must learn control, must become more self-reliant, if we want to make progress in life. Then, when we have learnt to cope with the trials and tribulations that we all have to face, when we have made strenuous efforts to avoid the pitfalls and to scale the heights, we will be rewarded with the Chariot of Success.

No. 8 – Justice

The mystery behind trump No. 8 needs explanation because the arcanum of this card reveals justice for what it really is – a balance of the forces known as cause and effect.

When we suffer what seems to be injustice in our personal lives we are really suffering from the effects of a cause we have put into motion ourselves. Though we may have acted in a certain way from the best of motives, we are often appalled at the apparent injustice of the sequel that follows our action. Yet it is not correct to claim that there is no justice in life, for there is.

What makes it appear unjust, however, is that the effects from a cause may be delayed and thus come as a shock to us. Often, we suffer the effects of our actions so much later that we have forgotten the cause that set them in motion. If we do someone an ill turn, we might seem to get away with it at the time because the scales are tipped in our favour; but the scales of justice must come to balance and, when they do, we reap the harvest of what we have done.

That is why, at times, we seem to suffer through the actions of others, even strangers. Yet the law of the balance is so subtle that our ill turn must come back to us at some time although it does not always come from the person to whom we did the ill turn in the first place. So the law of balance can and does operate through complete strangers.

Also, when the gods pronounce justice upon us it is not upon our actions but upon the motives that inspired those actions. Other people may regard us as lords and ladies of bounty and praise our good deeds, but the gods see the real motives that inspired those deeds. For instance, if we did a good turn for someone because of the self-gratification that it brought us, we would be judged on that motive and would receive the reward of vanity.

On the other hand, if we committed a crime with the best intentions, we would be again judged by the motives and go unpunished by the gods, although perhaps not by our fellow men! This is why some people who are outwardly good and kind suffer dire misfortunes whereas others apparently benefit from undeserved good fortune. The world may not see our original sins and virtues, but the gods will and therefore deliver justice with cold impartiality.

So, to the world some people may appear to suffer unjustly yet, in the occult scale, their sins might weigh heavily. Tarot card No. 8 therefore signifies the initiation that takes place when we learn, for the first time, to see ourselves as we really are and to judge ourselves fairly, without self-justification. For, only when we have judged ourselves can we realise that we do not know enough to condemn others.

Instead, we are enabled to put ourselves in the place of the accused, to see that his limitations are much the same as our own, and so extend the understanding that we would want ourselves. Such understanding is known as mercy, which is why the figure of Justice on this card is invariably depicted as a female one, for Mercy is a woman or, in mundane terms, has feminine traits.

In ancient Egyptian symbolism, the eighth card of the Major Arcana was known as the Scales of Ma'at and depicted a soul being judged in the Halls of Amenti, the Egyptian underworld where souls went after death. The soul was placed in one scale and weighed against the Feather of Truth while ibis-headed Thoth, the Recorder of man's life and deeds, stood by with his records.

In the ancient Egyptian tradition, the Scales of Ma'at were not only used to weigh the soul after death but also at certain other times during the individual's lifetime. And, according to which way the balance fell, he or she would receive a period of fortune or misfortune. A time of trial and tribulation, a period of worldly ordeal, was considered to be in repayment for injustices committed by that individual to others or, alternatively, was retribution for those deeds which had not yet been repaid.

Every evil thing we do or unfair advantage we take, if done knowingly, has to be paid for sooner or later. Sometimes the weighing in the balance follows soon after the deed; at other times it comes years later, which is far worse because the deed lies like a time-bomb waiting for the feather of retribution to set it off. That is where Thoth, the Egyptian recording angel, comes in with his little book because he was believed to record every good and every bad deed of a person's life.

It was he who had these deeds weighed against the feather of truth in the Scales of Ma'at, both during the subject's lifetime and after. Thoth recorded not only the deed itself but also the chain of events that it set in motion because an evil deed can have its effect on innocent lives apparently unconnected with the original perpetrator. Yet the culprit who sets such causes and effects in motion must, some day, pay the penalty for the whole.

Many evil or unkind actions find their retribution in life itself, so the judgement after death may be lenient. But, where the penalty has not been paid in this life, justice is stringent and the karma (debt) to be paid in the individual's next life on earth is heavy indeed. This was the philosophy behind the Scales of Ma'at and when we, in our turn, experience trials and ordeals that seem unfair, we should perhaps not ask 'Why should this happen to me?' but 'What was it that I did to merit this situation?'

If you believe in reincarnation, then any ordeal or injustice you have suffered may be karmic, but do not be in too much of a hurry to judge it so without first considering what might have set the Scales in motion during this life. It is also important to realise that earthly justice is administered by man and his laws may be quite different from the justice that is meted out by higher powers.

A judge in a law court can only deliver a fair verdict on a case as it has been presented to him and on the evidence submitted after both sides have placed themselves in their best light; the justice of higher powers, however, delivers its verdict on the case as it is known, with nothing hidden. Thus man may deceive himself and others, but he cannot deceive the gods.

So, when the card of Justice turns up in a spread, it is always a sign that the querent is about to receive justice and that it will be a heaven-sent judgement. Such a judgement will be in the querent's favour if the cards supporting card No. 8 are good, but it will go against him if they are cards of ill omen.

If the judgement does not go in his favour, this is when the querent needs mercy; and this will follow if he accepts the verdict, decides to cope with the situation, learns to do so and starts afresh having learned the lessons of this Tarot trump. For mercy lies behind justice and an end of one thing is the start of another; better things can lie around the corner.

No. 9 – The Hermit

Number 9 in the Tarot, the Hermit, can be interpreted as man in search of himself, starting on the long journey to find his own soul by retiring into himself. That is why, in most packs, he is depicted as a venerable old man carrying a lantern and supporting himself by a stout staff.

The lighted lantern represents any knowledge that he already has, plus faith in whatever creed he practises: it is the light by which he hopes to find the truth. The staff signifies the experience on which he has to lean and he is old because our souls are as old as time. Beneath his mantle, the Hermit is naked and unprotected – as is every soul; for truth is found not in external things or the experiences of others but from within ourselves.

So, the meaning of this card becomes clear, it represents mankind thrown in upon itself, searching for the soul, that spark of the eternal which is within each of us. But there is a deeper arcanum behind this card. The Hermit also stands for the awakened occultist who suddenly realises that he is utterly alone. For that is one of the drawbacks that initiation brings – you are no longer one of the herd.

Although you may live, work and play among a crowd, inside you is a secret lonliness because you are set apart by your actions and studies. The very possession of a certain amount of occult wisdom brings its own dangers – the fear that your delving into the unknown arouses in others who do not follow the same line of study. The modern would-be initiate has no temple to shield him but is open to every mischief that fearful or spiteful minds can devise: it is not devils of which he must beware but his fellow men.

All of us want to find truth, yet few of us can bear to face its stark reality, especially if is about ourselves. It is for this reason that we shun real self-analysis; we fear what we may discover in our secret hearts and dread to reveal the selfish motives that lie behind so many of our actions. It can be very hard to live with ourselves if we have been honest for there is no escape: we cannot run away from our own natures as we can from people and situations.

Constructive self-analysis leads to that wisdom and prudence which are symbolised by card No. 9, but self-justification leads to fear and excess caution which express themselves in doubts about the motives of others. Sadly, we often meet those who continually make excuses for themselves, who attribute the loftiest motives to even the meanest actions while blindly refusing to make excuses for the failings of others. Of course, such people deceive no one but themselves – but this is the greatest deception of all and must be paid for by continual bewilderment at what they consider to be the unfairness of life.

Yet the majority of our troubles are self-induced; they arise from inherent faults in our natures which we either do not recognise or which we gloss over and refuse to tackle. According to psychologists, our thoughts, actions, fears, hopes and dreams are hidden in our subconscious minds, ready to be drawn out by those with the necessary skills. We all have such skills and the never-ending attempt of humanity to have light shed on the darkness of itself is one of the fundamental causes of the study of the occult and its kindred arts.

As soon as anyone starts to ask 'who am I?' or 'what am I?' he has reached the stage of development signified by No. 9 in the Tarot, the Hermit. A hermit is a person who voluntarily elects to live apart from his fellow men, either because he finds their companionship wearisome or because he is at odds with them, somehow out of step, and wants to know why.

The moment you really want to know what you are, why you exist or what force impelled you into this world at the specific point at which it did, you can be compared to the Hermit, the lone-seeker who, by the light of that knowledge which he possesses, goes out into the darkness of his own ignorance to try and find an answer.

Yet the main factor that prevents man from discovering the knowledge within himself – the master that dwells within – is mankind. We fill our lives with canned music, canned voices, hour after hour, and deaden our sensibilities. No living soul should ever be compelled, at all hours of the day and night, to have the constant companionship of other humans. It is soul-destroying because it cripples the ability to think and reason; it destroys the deeper things within us and, too often, the affairs of others will impinge upon our own.

Everyone needs to set aside at least some part of the day when they can be by themselves, even if only in a public place among strangers to whom they need not speak; for being alone is not a physical but a mental state. The ability to be alone – and like it – is a great boon, it is an accomplishment. The sages knew this, which is they they became hermits. When one is away from the sounds of man, one can hear the voice of nature, the music of the spheres.

Yet being alone is not the same as loneliness. Real loneliness can be a distressing factor in anyone's life because it is the feeling of being unwanted; it is being on one's own without sufficient companionship or interests to keep one fully occupied. Those who fall in this category, who long to be in the midst of friends or family but are prevented by circumstances from so being, are represented by the Hermit reversed in a spread. This is why this card signifies timidity and fear when reversed: it is the fear of being lonely rather than choosing to be alone.

Yet what the lonely lack is illumination of themselves and ancient wisdom maintains that if we seek anything within ourselves, we will find it. When all outside help has fled, all comforts gone, we can draw strength from within ourselves – if we but try. To learn how to draw upon this mysterious strength, to know what it is and why it exists, is the true purpose of occultism. A true occultist wants to find out the meaning of life itself, and how its rules apply.

Often, the finest occultists are produced through some shattering experience which drives them within themselves, there to find the Mother of Wisdom to replace the lost, comforting 'Mummy' of childhood. Trials, tribulations and ordeals – even unhappiness – are all part of growing up. One does not become an adult simply by attaining a certain age, be it eighteen or twenty-one. The day we really become adult is when we stop merely running after what we want and decide what it is we must have or must accept. That is the true understanding of oneself.

In the last analysis, it is seldom the things we want that turn out to be best for us. It is as though, through being frustrated in our lives, and even in our emotions, we are able to find ourselves. Once we have done that, we are on our way to finding the universe and the gods: this is the arcanum of the Hermit.

No. 10 – The Wheel of Fortune

Number 10 of the Tarot trumps, the Wheel of Fortune, represents the ever-changing aspects of our lives – the various trials and tribulations we all have to face at one time or another, also the good fortune that comes our way at other times. It signifies the changing pattern of our lives, the alternating good and bad fortune which we encounter on the journey from birth to death.

It represents the cosmic wheel, with all the universes and their planets turning together; also our own universe with its ever-wheeling planets. Thus it symbolises the world as it turns beneath the unchanging stars which shed their light on humanity, affecting them for good or ill according to their capacity to deal with life.

Whether or not you believe in astrology, much occult teaching is founded upon it, and upon the assumption that the vibrations of the stars strike a response from mankind. Thus we are all tied to the wheel of earthly life and, as it turns, receive the benefits or tribulations meted out by the stars. Luck and misfortune seem to pursue us in a regular sequence yet, once we have learned to battle with, or adapt ourselves to the less fortunate aspects of life, we discover that it is our troubles that have taught us most and that, properly handled, they can bring fortunate changes in their train.

Allegorically, the Wheel of Fortune represents the Round Table of the Arthurian legends. No one Knight was elevated above another at this table, yet each knew that he would have to meet trial and danger, and resolve to meet it in his own way. The parallel with our present-day existence is plain: the successful ones among us are those who have learned to understand themselves and the powers within them which, properly used, enable mankind to control his life instead of being controlled by it.

The Wheel of Fortune is therefore regarded as a significant card in a divinatory spread because it presages change, which can be fortunate or otherwise according to its placement. In the mystic Tarot, however, it denotes the forces that work through mankind, some of which are under his control and some of which are not. Basically, it is a solar emblem but, to understand its arcana one must consider its deeper symbolism.

According to the Babylonian mysteries, this wheel had the Sun as its hub and its spokes symbolised the days of the solar year. At those points on the wheel's rim where the spokes touched it were spikes, above each of which was a magical sigil. Occupying each corner of the card was another symbol – the lion, eagle, man and bull which correspond to the Four Pillars of Earth and to the four seasons. This card was, therefore, a celestial wheel, a symbolic map of the heavens, and was used for divinatory purposes – it was an early system of astrology.

This system was based on the principle that the universe apparently revolved around the Sun and that the spikes on the wheel's rim would, therefore, point in turn to different celestial bodies each day of the year. If a straight line could be drawn from the wheel's hub (the Sun) along a spoke to any heavenly body, then that particular celestial sphere was considered to affect the luck of the day according to its nature, both in general terms and in personal affairs.

The interpretation of each day's spoke position was a complicated mathematical procedure based on magic, mysticism and magnetism, yet it probably formed the basis of that art which developed into astrology as we know it today. There are also astrological undertones to the symbolism depicted on the Wheel of Fortune cards in those packs which are based on the Egyptian mysteries.

Such cards depict the wheel turning on its axis, revolving eternally as does our planet in space, and at its summit is a sphinx armed with a drawn sword. To the right of the wheel is Anubis (more often shown as a fox or jackal in modern packs), one of the lesser gods in the Egyptian pantheon, whose function was to guide the souls of the dead through the halls of Amenti (the underworld) to the throne of Osiris for judgement. Counterbalancing Anubis on the other side of the wheel is Set (the devil), who is usually represented as a monkey on more modern cards.

Each corner of the card represents a Tarot card, each signifying a different property. In the top left-hand corner is the Ace of Cups, symbolising the chalice containing the elixir of life and wisdom; the top right-hand corner, the Five of Pentacles, signifying material benefit; the bottom left-hand corner, Ace of Swords, denoting occult power; and the bottom right-hand corner, Ace of Wands (or Staves), symbolising material experiences.

These four corners have an arcane significance, too, for they represent the 4th House of any individual's horoscope; his childhood environment and his ultimate end. In Egyptian astrology, the 4th House was known as the grave and referred to death – physical death and the termination of events. It was considered that the planets that occupied this House and any aspects made to them or to the House cusp indicated the major obstacles in life which the individual had to overcome because these things had been inherited from a former life.

The ancient Egyptians believed that physical death was only one link in an endless chain of cause and effect; thus the grave that held the physical body after one life was also the womb of the life yet to come. So card No. 10, the Mystic Wheel, was the great symbol of reincarnation and referred to matters of life and death.

In all ancient drawings, man as a living soul was depicted as a head only between two wheels; this symbolism refers to the wheel of life and death, also to that other wheel which we have all experienced, the Wheel of Fortune. The arcane law of this wheel is the law of changing fortunes. Mankind's life-span is one wheel, inside which are various wheels of change, each having its own periodicity which can be worked out roughly by our calendar system. Termination or changing points come into our lives every four, eight, twelve, sixteen, twenty-two and thirty years, as you will discover if you look back to significant points in your own life.

This law of the wheels is designed to provide us with change so that we develop our resources and initiative. Nobody ever finds that their whole life runs smoothly and that nothing bad ever happens; changes, both good and bad, come to us all. Yet, on balance, if we add up the gains of the good years against the losses of the bad ones, we come out even because there are powerful, arcane laws of compensation and retribution.

So, let the past go – it cannot be relived and it is the present and the future that are for living. Live one day at a time and concentrate on getting the best out of that one day. By so doing you will find yourself moving more easily into the future and you will be working with card No. 10 in the Tarot and not against it.

No. 11 – Strength

Strength, or Fortitude as it is sometimes called, is placed as No. 8 in some Tarot packs but as No. 11 in others. I favour the eleventh position because, if the Wheel of Fortune (No. 10) has not turned in one's favour, this card implies recovery after difficulties and victory over obstacles of any kind. It is therefore one of the most uplifting cards in the Tarot and, even if it falls reversed in a spread, cannot be regarded as a bad omen because its keynote is victory after struggle.

When this card appears in a spread, it signifies that the querent will have the fortitude or endurance to cope with any situation with which he or she may be faced. This interpretation is particularly pertinent if the card is reversed because it signifies that the difficult period has not yet been reached but lies in the near future.

The querent needs, therefore, to reconsider his aims and objectives for he could be applying his energies to the wrong ends. It may, for instance, mean that his natural gifts or abilities are not being channelled correctly and he may lose heart or waste energy in the pursuit of his objectives. Yet we all have untapped reservoirs of courage, strength, endurance or fortitude – call it what you will – within us upon which we can draw in times of trial and these traits are signified by the card called Strength.

If upright in a spread, it indicates that the hidden resources within the querent are already at work to overcome the obstacle, no matter what this may be, because this card refers to mental, physical and spiritual strengths. In most packs, Strength is symbolised by a young woman gripping a lion by its jaws and, in older packs, a warrior is shown defending his life against a savage beast – sometimes a lion, sometimes a tiger. In either case, the card's message is the same: rely on the strength within and have faith that it will not let you down and you will overcome all obstacles.

In divination, then, this card represents invincible strength and dauntless courage, with victory to those who know how to direct their wills into the right channels. However, like all the Tarot trumps, it has deeper meanings and in the Egyptian mysteries was considered to be one of the arcana of healing – self-healing with the aid of divine power – and this card is still associated with health and healing.

The lion is the solar emblem of physical life and is symbolic of strength; it therefore stands for the physical frame of man, within which he functions, and which may be strong or weak. Thus, when the lion turns and attacks man, it represents the body's weaknesses or diseases, which one must fight just as the warrior fights the leaping lion on this card.

When we have faith in the treatment we receive for our ailments and believe that we shall get better, we usually do; and, the more faith one has in ultimate recovery, the sooner it occurs. Stories of people who have triumphed over terrible physical handicaps are quite common and such people may be said to have conquered the leaping lion. They exemplify fortitude and faith, and demonstrate that these two powers can overcome most of life's obstacles; for it is important to realise that strength of mind is as important, if not more important than bodily strength.

The lion on this Tarot trump also represents all the fears by which mankind is beset; its roars are the feelings that threaten us – our apprehensions concerning life. Yet humanity only fears the unknown. It can cope with known horrors but fears that which is not understood; and with fear comes the first onset of self-defeat. Card No. 11's message is that there is nothing to fear once you have faced the truth, for accepting any ordeal that lies ahead and determining to do your best about it wins half the battle.

Once the mind is determined on this course, there comes a feeling of power and security from outside oneself – the power that is always at hand to help those who are prepared to help themselves. Nothing is ever as bad as fear seems to depict it and all ordeals can be gone through and triumphed over if one is honest with oneself. Self-honesty also reduces the trials that may lie ahead because it enables us to overcome those weaknesses of character that attract tribulations to us.

After all, why should any of us assume that we are among the small proportion of humanity for whom life is really tough? The odds are against it and, if only we think constructively, we can ensure against such an eventuality. We must learn to use our inner strength, to tell ourselves that every setback we overcome is another one behind us; we must believe that every day that we live we will become wiser and better able to cope with life's daily trials.

But, if we think negatively, if we sit back and wait for life's problems to overwhelm us because we are too weak to face the challenge, then we have no one but ourselves to blame when the future looks bleak. Our inner strength will seem to wane if we accept in advance that those things which we don't want to happen are bound to come our way. Yet this isn't so and will only happen if we let it because we all possess the necessary faith and fortitude, wisdom and experience to get on top of any troubles – such qualities are those symbolised by the Tarot trump called Strength.

Fortunately for us all, selfish and cowardly as we may be when faced with an ordeal, we have a higher side that won't really let us rest complacently if we have dodged the issue. So, give it a chance because you will find that even the greatest ordeal will shrink to manageable proportions when you have summoned the warrior angel – spiritual strength – to fight by your side. That is the deeper meaning behind this card.

The young woman shown closing the jaws of the roaring lion with such ease and lack of fear symbolises the soul; the female form is used because the soul was always depicted as feminine. Above her head is the same 'figure eight' halo-like symbol as is shown above the head of the male figure on Tarot trump No. 1, the Magician (in some packs, both figures wear hats of the same design), a card which is strongly linked with this one.

In the arcanum of the Tarot, each trump is considered to be a development or continuation of another because each card represents a step on the occult way; each signifies a stage in the soul's journey – its initiatory progress. Thus, just as the Magician signifies awareness of inner powers – the magical powers that the initiate must learn to develop – strength also refers to these powers and denotes that the initiate has reached the stage of understanding how they can be used in his search for truth.

So, the card called Strength denotes those inner resources that we all possess and the development of the higher self through spiritual powers rather than magical ones; it is the development of the psyche rather than the employment of the forces of nature (signified by the Magician); it denotes mental and physical health and spiritual potential – perfect balance.

No. 12 – The Hanged Man

The twelfth card in the Major Arcana, the Hanged Man, represents trials, vicissitudes and, above all else, self-denial and personal sacrifice. If this card falls reversed in any position in a divinatory spread, it indicates that any such self-sacrifice will be wasted. We are all obviously and quite rightly called upon to make sacrifices for others from time to time, but the main function of this card is to indicate the possible outcome of a particular sacrifice demanded at a certain time.

So, when called upon to make such a sacrifice, you are advised to see whether or not the Hanged Man turns up in a Tarot spread. It is important to realise, however, that when the figure of the young man on the cross-tree is shown hanging down, this card is upright and, when his foot points to the ground, it is reversed: it's a case of wrong way up is right!

The ancients said that a self-sacrificing person (meaning one who is constantly yielding to others) is looking at life from an upside-down position because he imagines that he is benefiting others by putting their interests before his own. This in fact may be the case for there are certainly occasions when it is so, but before sacrificing oneself for a cause or another person, there is a point that should be considered.

Are you not, by taking on another person's burden, preventing him learning from experience and being over-protective? Or are you, perhaps, even enjoying the fact that he will be placed under a deep emotional or practical obligation? These are very real dangers and it is important, therefore, to examine one's motives honestly before making a great sacrifice for anyone, especially if by doing so one completely robs the other person of his right to pay for his own mistakes.

We all make mistakes, but we have a moral obligation to pay for these ourselves and not to place their burden on others' shoulders. So, instead of making continual, fruitless self-sacrifices, we should strive to help others to help themselves and reserve self-sacrifice for really vital issues. To help others you have to sacrifice time, trouble and material things – which is acceptable – but to sacrifice yourself continuously is wrong. Your own life, good name and the things you have earned are just as important for you as are these things for others.

Sometimes, of course, there are occasions when real self-sacrifice is necessary, when there is absolutely no other way to save somebody you love more dearly than you love yourself. Then it is valid and rates as a virtuous act, yet this sort of situation may occur only once in a lifetime. So, if it happens more than once, examine your own feelings and the motives behind them because you may be enjoying playing the martyr.

The basis of genuine sacrifice is love of some kind, whether of a person, an ideal or a belief, and its acceptance is always voluntary. Sacrifices that are forced on us are not sacrifices at all; real sacrifices are those we make voluntarily, accepting at the time we make them that there will be no reward as such. This implies a great step forward in soul development for it signifies that we have passed for ever the point where only self-interest rules our lives. We have, in fact, passed from spiritual childhood (for self-centredness is a childish trait) to the adulthood of voluntary choice.

Once the soul starts to develop, it does not stop, it grows each day and, with its growth, we become not only better people but more powerful ones, too. Sacrifice implies no self-interest, and to forget the self – if only for a time – is all to the good. We are all prisoners of our own natures and self-centredness, so to break away from the self occasionally revives us, just as water revives a drooping flower.

At the same time, this does not mean that the self-abnegating person who runs around looking for chances to sacrifice for anything and anyone has a more developed soul than anyone else – far from it. There is no point in such behaviour and one must not allow oneself to becomes a human doormat for the selfishness of others. For every giver there are a thousand takers, and to give (sacrifice) indiscriminately is foolish; one must use discretion because a bond is formed between giver and taker.

Perhaps the one for whom the sacrifice is made carries the harder burden because he knows and accepts the gift without being able to reciprocate. So, people should not allow others to sacrifice themselves for their sakes unless they are prepared to admit this bond, for there must be reciprocity at some time – if not in this life, then in the life to come, whether on a higher plane of existence altogether, or in some time of rebirth that brings the participants together again.

So, sacrifice of the self for another can bring inner peace that comes with an awakened soul. It may signify the way of thorns, the cross of tribulation and suffering, but it leads to the crown of spiritual attainment and the sword of power, which begins with self-mastery. Sacrifice makes an indelible impression on the records of time and forms a spiritual bond that lasts for ever.

Each of the Tarot trumps describes a particular state of occult development and the arcanum of the Hanged Man and trump Number 8, Justice, are linked. It signifies that man's judgement is often topsy-turvy (No. 12), but that the justice of the gods is impartial, balanced and inexorable (No. 8). Occult laws are those that keep universes in place – they work eternally with accuracy and justice; man's laws are those imposed upon him by religion, country and environment – they are only temporary.

Thus what is right by mundane, worldly laws is often wrong according to occult law; and this the would-be initiate had to understand. In trying to align man-made ideas of justice and mercy with the occult laws, the initate had to grasp a new perception of right and wrong – and this stage of his development is well represented by the Hanged Man, symbolising the awakened seeker. He is not totally free of the material world for he is tied by one foot to a pole balanced between two uprights (a gibblet) and is therefore still dependent on the physical world; yet his upside down position signifies his reversal of this dependency for coins can fall from his pockets, symbolising his rejection of materialistic values.

The suspended figure's eyes are wide open and spiritual triangles are formed in the spaces between his legs, arms and body, signifying that he has turned his eyes to the heavens, is spiritually aware, and has a new perspective on the earthly world. He has attained a degree of arcane knowledge through his earthly trials and temptations and has learned the spiritual rewards of self-denial and sacrifice.

No. 13 – Death

The most unnecessarily hideous card of the Tarot trumps is No. 13, sometimes called the Grim Reaper but more often known as Death. Because of its title, illustrators of the past have, naturally, associated this card with human dissolution and it usually depicts a skeletal figure, either scything ground littered with heads, hands, feet and bones or else wearing armour and riding a horse that is stepping through the mortal remains that litter the ground.

It acquired its dire symbolism in medieval times and would have been better illustrated by a serpent with its tail in its mouth to signify that in the end is the beginning, for that is what this card really means. Therefore, when this card appears in a spread it does not necessarily signify the physical death of someone but simply the end of something – often the matter a sitter is enquiring about – and all things have a beginning and an end.

So, if you shuffle and cut the Tarot trumps and card No. 13 turns up, it signifies that the question in your mind when you cut the cards has already been decided: whatever it is – whether a relationship, situation or particular set of circumstances – the thing is at an end. It is as simple as that and there is no need to enquire into the matter further. It is important that trump No. 13 should not be feared or misunderstood because it is, essentially, a card signifying new beginnings.

The members and bones through which the Reaper's scythe cuts its swathe are no more than pictorial emblems of our daily lives. There is, for instance, the work of the hands which, eventually, comes to an end; the work of the head – thoughts and plans – must end, too, before the action needed to put these things into effect can begin. The scythe is a symbol of travelling and therefore represents journeys that have been accomplished; and the bare bones are no more then the unwanted residue of any thing or any matter which has had its time and now must end.

There is no need for despondency at the implied end of something if one remembers that, before new beginnings, old things have to end.

For instance, existing buildings have to be pulled down before new ones can be built; old clothes have to be discarded in order to make room for new ones. When things come to the end of their usefulness, so far as you are concerned, you are then ready to turn your attention to other matters.

This card has another name, Lord of the Gates, and these gates symbolise day and night, light and darkness – the beginning (life) and termination (death) of all things. Ancient lore teaches us that there are stations in life at which the Lord of the Gates exercises his terminating influence over the affairs of man and when such important changes in our lives are due card No. 13 usually turns up in a spread. It signifies a time of change and, more often than not, when this card occurs in a Tarot reading it denotes a complete change of circumstances for the enquirer.

Matter of any kind is indestructible; only its form can change. For instance, things that are apparently completely consumed by fire combine in the atmosphere as chemicals and thus play their part in furthering new growth: they have not died but have been transmuted. Man himself undergoes changes and transformations throughout his life; we all begin as seeds, develop, mature and, in time, will be cut down and transformed into another kind of life.

The idea of transmutation lay at the very heart of the ancient Egyptian traditions. It was the underlying principle behind their belief that death was not the end of life but the beginning of a new and better state; a mere laying aside of one fleshy envelope to await the donning of another, with a long-awaited rest on the other side (the Halls of Amenti) after judgement had been pronounced. Their attitude to death was unique because, as a nation, they built and planned not for life but for death and the after-life.

To the ancient Egyptians, death was no grim reaper but a welcome visitor for which even the poorest member of society prepared. Although most of their religions tended towards a belief in reincarnation, the obsession with death and what lay beyond it dominated the Egyptian mind above everything else. So, when we come to consider what the thirteenth card of the Major Arcana really signifies in Tarot divination, we must align our minds with Egyptian philosophy and regard death simply as representing a transition from one form of existence to another.

Occultism teaches people to accept quite simply that we are born and must die; that is one cycle. Within it are others, such as those of love, luck, health, prosperity and adversity. Card No. 13 marks the ends of cycles and is, therefore, associated with Chronos, God of Time. Chronos is also another name for Saturn which, again, is but another name for The Reaper; and the corn must be mown or scythed before it can be ground into flour to make bread, without which man cannot live. So, this card is not of ill omen but signifies time, the end of one cycle and, more importantly, the beginning of a new one.

Between birth and death we have a span of time – that precious possession which, if squandered, can never be recaptured. Probably the greatest time-waster is worrying about the future; people who worry about the future or dwell in the past are wasting the present: today is the future we worried about yesterday. Then, if all is going well today, we worry about the possibility of it going wrong tomorrow – how futile! We should not waste our time and our lives alike; we all have our allotted span in which to live, learn and make something of our stay here on earth.

The mystic understands this and accepts the inevitability of change, for it is part of life and nothing is static. It is unreasonable to expect that nothing will ever change; we ourselves change all the time. We are not even the same people today as we were yesterday because time itself changes. We all go through cycles of little deaths and little births as the pattern of our lives evolve. We gain, in some way, from each one of these, we develop after each experience.

The person who has been shielded from the knocks and hardships of life never learns self-reliance and, because of that lack, other qualities cannot develop. The person to whom recurring misfortunes happen should therefore ask himself what it is he has to learn, for these changes, or little deaths, do not occur without reason: they are intended to be part of our development.

This is the message of the card called Death: changes are necessary. Endings must come before beginnings, just as the pre-natal life of a child ends at the moment of birth when it draws its first breath and becomes a separate human being with its own destiny before it.

No. 14 – Temperance

The fourteenth card in the Major Arcana is a fortunate card, signifying fruitfulness – the replenishment or provision of that which may be lacking in the enquirer's life. It also represents action, life and vitality, tempered with wisdom and restraint, hence it is known as Temperance.

The symbolism depicted on this card – a winged (and therefore angelic) figure pouring water from one vessel into another in equal parts – expresses the main arcanum behind this trump. Temperance equates to the middle way – enough of everything but neither a lack nor a surplus of anything. The transference of water from one vial to another symbolises movement, so the message of this card becomes clear; it signifies that all good things come from temperance and movement.

Movement brings change and, although rest and repose are vital, idleness brings stagnation, which in turn breeds boredom and dissatisfaction. On the other hand, opportunities arise as a result of events that are set in motion and which bring changes in their wake. So, part of the message behind this card is that too much leisure fills the vessel of idleness whereas energy, work and applied effort fill the vessel of attainment.

Keeping things on the move is the secret of success, of attainment and an interesting life. When you work at something or attempt anything, you are contributing positively towards the realisation of your wishes and desires, no matter how unconnected with your eventual aims such action may appear to be. Your actions will set events in motion and then opportunities can occur. But if you just wait for things to happen, if you take a negative attitude and simply do nothing, this is exactly what will occur – nothing!

Yet vitality and action can degenerate into restlessness and instability if taken to excess – and temperance is the antithesis of excess. So there is an inherent warning in this card. When it falls reversed in a divinatory spread, it warns the enquirer that, although life may soon become rosier, it will not remain that way for long if abundance of any kind is allowed to cause his better characteristics to degenerate.

Some people, for instance, may allow themselves and their lives to be ruined by riches. This is because plenitude degenerates into dissolution if temperance is not observed and if spendthrift tendencies are encouraged rather than curbed. Similarly, a person who likes to drink may allow that enjoyment to degenerate into drunkenness if there is an abundance of liquor around, whereas the same situation would not tempt the teetotaller at all. So, as with all Tarot readings, the nature, habits and personal circumstances of the enquirer must be taken into consideration before deciding what effect this card will have on his life.

Despite the implicit warning contained in this card when it appears reversed in a spread, it is basically a fortunate omen. When everything in life seems to have come to a stop – when there is no movement, no change, and life has become a chore or a bore – Temperance can represent a beneficial change in one's life, particularly if it falls upright.

Although known as Temperance, this Tarot trump has an arcane name, Daughter of the Reconcilers, which we should consider if we are to comprehend just a fraction of its deeper meaning. It is important in this respect that the essential symbolism of this card has been retained: the female figure pouring fluid from one vessel to another does so without spilling a drop.

We all have cause to bless those people who reconcile us with others whom we have offended or with whom we have been at odds. The fluid being poured from one vessel to another on this card expresses symbolically what such people do: they take our best intentions and convey these to those we have offended, presenting all the factors in the best possible light, thus bringing about reconciliations through mediation.

Such people are well represented by this card's arcane title, Daughter of the Reconcilers; but, on a deeper level, it also signifies the mediators or reconcilers between earth and the higher planes, the Angels of Justice, which is why the figure depicted on this card is usually shown as winged. On this level, the fluid symbolises the water of life and the two vessels represent the giver of life, the creator, and the acceptor of life, mankind.

The giver of life also gave us certain rules, or laws, by which our lives should be lived if we are to get the best from them and, at the same time, adjured us to give of our best to make the world a better place in which to live. Sadly, however, most of us are acceptors and few are givers. It is human nature, unfortunately, to act primarily from selfish motives and, too often, we fail to pour something of what we have into the vessel of another who is in need of that which we possess.

There are, of course, some self-sacrificing people in the world but, more often than not, their sacrifices are made only for members of their families or for friends, which is not enough. We all need to learn to give of ourselves – our time, knowledge and substance – to those outside our immediate circles: to do at least one good turn without expectation of reward, to help humanity in general.

Such an action will, in fact, be repaid over and over again, though not necessarily by the person for whom the good deed was done and, perhaps, in quite unexpected ways, because no effort made for others is ever wasted. It is an occult law that when you least expect it, or most need it, you will be rewarded for your previous good action and that it will be enhanced and multiplied. Yet even in this – the doing of good deeds – your action should be tempered by moderation, as with anything signified by this card.

Temperance implies moderation, patience, calmness and freedom from selfish motives, so one must first judge who can be beneficiaries of your good deeds. This is important because the world is full of weaklings looking for somebody to shoulder their burdens and to help such folk is merely to increase their helplessness. It is better to advise them how to shoulder their own burdens than to assume them yourself or such people will never learn how to cope with life.

Patience is needed because people almost always seem to resent it if you do them a good turn. Such resentment does not usually last, however, for it arises from a temporary feeling of inferiority on the part of those who have received help from another. The calmness of acceptance is necessary, too, if you are let down by those for whom you have made sacrifices. Remember, there will be others who, at some time in the future, will be the means of repaying what has been given.

Freedom from selfish motives is essential when helping others because it raises us – however temporarily – to the level of the angels. We do not feel self-righteous but are uplifted because we have achieved something important; we have transferred some of our bounty from our vessel into that of another without spilling a drop, so our effort has not been wasted.

No 15 – The Devil

Major Arcana card No. 15 is called the Devil for want of a better name. The Devil was said to have many aspects, or faces, and he also had another name, Temptation, which is, perhaps, a better one for defining what this Tarot card represents because many of the evils that befall mankind are the results of temptation of one kind or another.

So, whenever this card appears in a spread, no matter what position it occupies, it must be regarded as a warning that the enquirer is soon to become the victim of an overwhelming temptation which, if not resisted, will bring a train of evil in its wake. When reversed, it signifies that this temptation will come with such a vast, malign power that the querent is likely to stand little chance of resisting it.

The Devil works on the weaknesses of mankind, which is why it signifies temptation; we are tempted with that which we most desire and thus it is very difficult to resist. The two figures depicted on this card are shown chained to the Devil – a Satanic figure seated on a throne – and represent man and woman (the opposing sides of one's nature) standing against the powers of darkness. The figures are usually shown naked, signifying that they are unarmed, but are fettered by their gross, material desires.

In many religions the Devil was not considered to be an evil power and he was worshipped by many of the ancient civilisations. The ancient Egyptians, for example, worshipped the Devil under the name of Set and did not regard him as malign; it was only Set's negative side, Typhon, that was considered to be a destroyer. Thus the horned god of the Tarot, which is strongly associated with the passions and weaknesses of mankind, corresponds to Typhon, the negative, destructive element that abides in all living creatures.

The ancients were not so foolish as to believe that even the wisest of us were safe from the tempter's power for they believed that mankind had within himself the very weaknesses that must, eventually, lead to his destruction. For it is a truth that a person in the grip of an overwhelming temptation can never be reasoned with but must be taught to reason with himself; and this, then, is the lesson that must be learned from Tarot card No. 15.

It must, therefore, be obvious that if this card turns up in a divinatory spread, care should be taken in interpreting it for the enquirer. Some people cannot bear the truth and, as this card also implies suffering a temporary imbalance, great caution is required because the querent may react violently and fly into a rage, deny the implications categorically or become deeply depressed or distressed as a result of the interpretation.

The temptations implied by this card and its likely consequences are so malign that little can be said in its favour. Interpreters should, therefore, bear in mind that they could be opening the flood-gates of hell when they interpret this card and should seek for ameliorating conditions; the other cards in the spread should be studied carefully in order to offset the more depressing aspects of card No. 15.

So, we have to be somewhat careful in definng the real danger of the Devil, a card which, more than anything, warns of the dire consequences of failing to resist the temptations of the flesh. For sexual desire can be so strong at times that it turns the victim into a self-destructive fool, unable to resist temptation even if this results in his downfall.

Yet, in such a permissive society as exists today, the dire warning of this card might be ignored unless it can be explained at an occult level and, in order to do that, we must look to the mysteries for an answer. In this sense, trump No. 15 represents kundalini, the serpent fire. This fire is believed to be linked to the spinal fluid which, mounting, feeds the brain and results in great mental activity, inspiration and, sometimes, even a flash of sheer genius.

When the serpent fire is reversed or flowing downwards, however, it stirs up the sexual appetites of the person concerned to such a degree that it renders him temporarily unbalanced mentally. People in such a condition think, as it were, with their sexuality instead of with their brains. Fortunately, this reversal of kundalini does not occur often but, when it does, the victims become their own executioners. They become prey to infatuations so demanding that they throw away their honour, career, family and life itself rather than separate from the desired one.

Reversed kundalini is the veritable 'temptation of the devil' that ancient literature frequently alludes to but never defines. Once aroused, it is difficult to quell; it is like a raging fire in the blood which cannot be stilled until the fire has consumed all that lies in its path, even the mental or physical health of the victim. The victim will descend to an abyss from which he cannot extricate himself until all passion is spent; and it is as well to remember that uncontrolled passions describe not only carnal lust but any overwhelming lust or greed, any powerful material temptation.

Fortunately, however, the serpent fire is rarely roused, few of us ever encounter absolute evil even though we have all known it in various lesser forms. But those of us who have met absolute evil, expressed either on the occult or physical plane, can never erase entirely from our minds the fearful impression that it leaves. Only when the individual spirit develops fully is it allowed to encounter the hierarchy and principalities of evil, for occult contestants must be evenly matched.

Yet man must have something to fight against; he must have evils – temptations – to overcome in order to develop his full powers. If he is not fighting evil on the right plane – the mental – he will have to deal with it on his own plane – the physical – and that can lead to war, oppression, all forms of tyranny and physical ills. Thus evil must exist in the world if humanity is to progress and each individual must learn to overcome his particular devil in order that his soul can develop.

The Devil and his cohorts are not all-powerful; they only have supreme power over those who fear them; and they are a necessary part of the occult scheme of things. Evil is good misplaced, a mighty power under the wrong control, which is why the Devil is referred to as the Lord of Misrule, he is lord of wrong application. Nothing in itself is evil and only by misuse does it become so. The power of the Devil therefore lies within ourselves and, when we learn how to use and not abuse everything on this earth, we have, in effect, conquered evil. We can then see the dreaded card No. 15 for what it really is, mankind's own ignorance, conceit and greed.

This card and its warnings should never be treated lightly, however, and any thoughts of 'getting away with it' should be put aside firmly. The Devil is a warning and appears when we are standing at one of life's cross-roads; and each individual must decide on the right path for himself.

No. 16 – The Tower Struck by Lightning

The sixteenth card in the Tarot trumps is one of the worst omened in the pack and, whenever it appears in a spread, its message portends unhappiness, deception, disgrace and ruin. The evil this card brings takes the form of a sudden and unforeseen calamity, whether it is reversed or not. I therefore advise interpreters to be very careful how they deal with any spread which contains this card because it can over-ride any good cards that also appear in the spread.

All wrongs that are comitted, whether by criminals, people in positions of power or by normal everyday people like you and me, have to be paid for sooner or later. When we knowingly do something wrong, we set in motion a series of causes and effects. The cause is what we actually do; the effect is what we might gain by the deed committed and an unlawful gain has another effect – what you most value will, in turn, be taken from you. The magnitude of that loss will be judged by the magnitude of the wrong that has been committed knowingly.

The warning of the Tower is dire indeed, and one ignores it at one's peril. Card No. 16 represents divine retribution – the hand of God – and strikes without warning, like a bolt from the blue. The Tower Struck by Lightning symbolises the biblical Tower of Babel which was erected by a powerful king, Nimrod, who was a mighty hunter. In his vanity (and vanity is always associated with the ruin wrought by the Tower) Nimrod thought that he could build a tower to reach to the heavens so that he could shoot his arrow into the Sun – the very eye of God.

The Sun represents ambition, often of an overweening kind, and this, when associated with wrongful pride (vanity), brings down the wrath of God. And just as the Tower of Babel was struck by lightning – the bolt from the blue, the hand of God – and crumbled into dust, so the plans of mankind, when wrong, overweening or just downright selfish, can be struck down by invisible lightning and end in ruins.

When the Tower of Babel was struck down, there were no pieces left big enough to pick up as it had crumbled into dust. Similarly, when man's edifices that are built on vanity are struck down, there is not enough left of the former life to make it worthwhile picking up the pieces. Those concerned in such a catastrophe are stricken physically, mentally, emotionally and materially. So, man is warned to beware of thinking he has everything under his control because, the moment he thinks that, fate, the gods, call it what you will, steps in to prove that he has not.

16 THE TOWER

Unexpected catastrophes occur in all our lives, often sweeping away loved ones, homes, fortunes and even reputations, leaving us to fight the world alone. When such an ordeal has happened, we are often too shattered to trust our own judgement of any situation or of ourselves. Yet these things happen for a purpose; they teach us through necessity that when friends desert us we must look upward for help – for it will come if we have learnt the Tower's lesson.

When an individual reaches that stage of development where the material assistance of friends and relations, or the possession of money and comfort, combine to halt the soul's upward struggle, then these things are swept away. And thus the individual must indeed stand alone; he must realise to the full that, far from being merely a comfortable member of a herd, he has to fight and think for himself.

Although he may touch the very depths materially, there comes the upswing; and with it comes greater spiritual knowledge and occult

111

power. Only then does man find that within himself he has the ability to triumph over the worst that life can do to him, that never again need he be haunted by that nameless fear of what may happen. The Tower eventually frees him from fear and, lacking fear, the hosts of darkness have no power over him.

When, in our lives, we encounter and triumph over the trials denoted by cards Nos. 15 and 16 of the Tarot, we have passed through two powerful tests and have become initiates of the Temple of Life — minor adepts permitted to wield the sword of power and truth. We have learned to use the power within us to overcome obstacles and evil. We know, too, the truth about life that it is a series of minor and major initiations and that all things can be overcome by the correct application of knowledge gained.

We all have to face our real trials alone and it is up to each of us to equip ourselves for the struggle both mentally and spiritually. After all, we first came into life alone, emerging from the cradling womb into the world with a cry of protest. We leave the world alone, too, for no friend may accompany us on death's journey. Why, then, should we fear to encounter alone any adventure that lies between those two points? For there is a beauty and an immeasurable comfort that comes from being able to say: 'It happened to me – and I conquered it, and learned from it.'

The Tower represents man, his achievements, his possessions, his status in the eyes of the world and his own soul. All of these can be destroyed at one fell swoop, save the soul. This should rise like the phoenix from the ashes of life's annihilation, be stronger and better from the trials through which it has passed, rebuilding life, career and everything else anew; and be more glorious than before. Thus, after life's structure has been razed to the ground, there should follow the rebuilding, assisted by occult or spiritual inspiration and help as symbolised by Major Arcana card No. 7, the Chariot.

But, if the initiate – the student magician – is found wanting in basic understanding, if he fails to learn life's lessons, this rebuilding does not take place. He then comes into conflict with the occult laws which can help man to soar, but only if his intention is to make this world a better place. They can, and will, raise him to the zenith of power providing that he holds this ideal before his eyes. But once let him falter in his dedication, once let him put himself and self-glorification before the ideal of helping the world, and those same powers will topple him to utter ruin.

The Tower uses each individual's personal weakness to destroy him: this is No. 16's ordeal. A man must face his own weakness and conquer it or be conquered by that very weakness. And, if the latter, he will be found wanting. But those who are not defeated rise from the depths to soar again, to rebuild life anew; and here they have the help of the Chariot.

Those who are now faced with the ruin of all they have built or striven for are offered the consolation symbolised by the seventh Tarot trump which represents help from above, occult inspiration and the path to the Sun. Look within yourself and see what is left to you and use this to rebuild your life; you will find that the desire and effort will be accompanied by divine inspiration and help. The gods are just, not cruel, and after the punishment comes help to rebuild. So, be strong and grasp the reins of your life again.

No. 17 – The Star

The seventeenth card in the Tarot trumps, the Star, is little understood. But the group of eight stars shown on this card offers the first clue to its inner arcana. Eight is the sum of 1 plus 7, or 17, the number of the Star; it is also the number of the trump called Justice.

We suffer because we are justly made to do so (No. 8, Justice). If we won't weigh ourselves in the balance, we are tried and weighed without our consent. The exact method of our initiation will, of course, differ in each individual case; which is why suffering so often appears unequal: the lash falls on each of us where it hurts most. Its purpose is to make us stronger; to make us rebuild ourselves, mentally and physically, into greater, wiser beings. That is the meaning of the eight stars on this card.

Occult knowledge and power are often the sequel to terrible personal experiences, the seeds of which we have usually sown ourselves through our actions, our natures, or by our inability to set right those faults we know we possess. The recognition and overcoming of our faults is an important occult lesson and, until we can do this, the greater secrets of the mysteries will not be unveiled to us. 'He who has not mastered himself can never master fate,' wrote a high priest of Amen-Ra.

Serious advocates for the adept's robe suffer the greatest initiations. When the gods give much, they must take much back; the less you know, the less you have and the less there is to lose. That is why the earthly tribulations of the non-aspiring are so much less severe: they suffer more as a group than as individuals. Thus we are led to the inner mystery of the Star.

The Star is hope; it tops the good fairy's wand; it is the symbol of Venus, the Lesser Fortune; it was the emblem of Bethlehem; and it was also the Morning Star, that Son of the Morning who was Lord of

Light– Lucifer, later known as Satan. The star, in fact, is concerned in all mystic truths and has its place in every religion.

When asked to visualise a star, most people imagine a five-pointed sigil: the pentagram, an important symbol in acquiring earthly power and which, when it has one point uppermost, represents man. So, someone who has sufferd the Tower's ruin, has been borne up and inspired by the Chariot and realises how he can do better, has reached the Gate of the Star. At last he understands that he can become master of his fate only when he has mastered the failings that brought him to ruin.

If you, too, have undergone a terrible trial, you now stand at the Gate and, just as Lucifer signified intellect without emotion, so, for a time, must let your mind and not your feelings rule you. Face the facts, cast out self-pity; grasp your fate and turn it into something entirely new and wonderful – like the star on top of the good fairy's wand. Then, like the initate in ancient Egypt, you will be able to face the future with new confidence and new powers.

You will shake the dust of the past from you when you tread the Way of the Star. And lighting that path into the dark unknown are the soft rays of Venus, the Lesser Fortune, the planet that brings happiness to mankind. Those who have suffered greatly, who have lost all and must now rebuild their lives, will have their path illuminated by that gentle star.

All they are asked to do is to put aside false emotions for a time and to use their intellects: to tread that path alone. They will then realise that the desolation wrought by the Tower's fall also carried away many former cares and worries. Battered and exhausted they may be, yet they will be reborn and, whatever their years, become again as little children.

Once embarked on the Way of the Star, no new problem will be presented until their mental and physical resources are rebuilt – all is hopeful. The oppressed are encouraged and helped by the gods and mankind alike. Inundated with the water of life, as Egypt was inundated by the Nile, they are regenerated.

The route is lovely and peaceful. Along it are found friends and helpers, inspiration and joy. It signifies the peace following tribulation that all initiates are allowed to enjoy; but there is no way through the Gate of the Star unless you have first suffered the agonies of the Tower. That is why the Gate is guarded by Sirius, the Dog-star, the watch-dog of the gods.

In old Egyptian packs, the female figure depicted on this card represents Isis; the two streams of water symbolise the regular flooding of the Nile through the two kingdoms (Upper and Lower Egypt) on which the well-being of the Land of Khemu depended; while the resplendent star surmounting the group of eight is Sirius, a star closely associated with the Egyptian mysteries. The bird on a tree, which in modern packs is shown as a dove, was an ibis – symbol of hope.

Hope, then, is the keynote of this card in a divinatory spread. Just as hope was reborn in Egyptian hearts when the tears that Isis shed for her dead husband, Osiris, caused the annual rising of the Nile that fertilised Egypt's arid lands. It also represents fresh hope and renewed courage, followed by the help of providence (the Chariot) that comes to the poor, battered soul who has endured the awful rigours of the Tower; and it marks the next step on the occult path.

The young woman depicted on card No. 17 is pouring water from two vessels into a spring, thus both her right and left hands are employed in her effort – the conscious and subconscious, her whole being. Above her head shines Sirius, the navigator's star, symbolising that our lives must be charted and planned, our whole efforts put into achieving our hopes, and that each of us must give our full contribution to the spring of life because we will only get out of it what we put in.

Great rewards only come after great efforts, great peace only after great pain; yet no situation ever occurs in life which leaves the individual bereft of hope. Secretly, no matter how materialistic we may be, we realise that beyond ourselves is a saving grace that can descend upon us. And No. 17 of the Tarot trumps, the Star, represents hope – the one vital element in life without which humanity cannot endure.

Always we hope, or we could not go on, which is why the arcanum of this card was regarded as very important by the initiates of old. Hope signifies regeneration, it is the water poured on the arid desert and which brings it to life. It is the mainspring of most of humanity's efforts; it is the shining star that glimmers above the path which leads to the Cup of Happiness. Happiness must be earned by self-analysis, the courage to face life and the will to fulfil dreams and ambitions.

No. 18 – The Moon

The eighteenth trump, the Moon, is a card which signifies much, but mainly that aspect of the Moon that is illusory. Study of the Moon's mysteries soon reveals a strange quality about this changeful orb which can inspire by aiding the imagination and also destroy by inflaming it. She is at once the Light of the Darkness, the Mother of Mysteries and the Lady of Illusion.

In one aspect, that of occult inspirer, the Moon represents constructive imagination and the true seer; but in another, the Mother of Unbalance, she is the begetter of harmful delusions, a state of mind that can range from mistaken idealism to downright lunacy. It is her capacity as the Lady of Illusion that is most concerned with this Tarot trump.

Each of us, at some time in our lives, has entered the temple of illusion. We all get crackpot ideas sometimes, and even pursue them. Fortunately for us, we see at last the error of our beliefs, but not before some harm has been done. To enter through the door of the temple of illusion usually means that you are due to be bound up in your illusions for a specific period. At its shortest, this will be one lunar month and, at its longest, two years; the most usual period, though, is nine lunar months.

There is however, one valuable lesson to be learned from the temple of illusion. It is that the mind, or imagination, can actually control the body and cause physical reactions. Doctors are well aware of this phenomenon and false pregnancies are well-known to them. Illusion-ruled people can have 'pregnancies' of other strange kinds, too.

For instance, some men have spent fortunes and their lives building follies: the world is full of pretentious buildings or 'follies' that have ruined their originators in mind, body and fortune. These are temples of illusion whose builders are driven to erect them by a strange power working within them. Seldom do such buildings serve any useful purpose: they are truly 'follies' of the Moon.

Yet even those of us who have not fortunes to expend on follies can still make our own temples of illusion. Sometimes we are convinced that someone who is not in the least interested in us is madly in love with us. The papers abound in stories of the excesses that people will go to when in the grip of this particular illusion. Others get the 'litigation bug'; they get a chip on their shoulder about something and spend their lives, energies and substance in one legal action after another, to gain a point that is itself based on imagination or delusion.

Illusions, however, can bring happiness too, even if only temporarily, and one should not try to destroy that happiness. When it vanishes by itself, as when the song of the Lorelei dies away, the ship of illusion will founder on the rocks. Illusion and delusion are, in any case, very difficult to deal with because they rule the mind through imagination – that same imagination which can inspire poets, painters, writers, architects and musicians. The Moon has many moods and some of them can be inspiring.

So be gentle with illusions for they will yield with time; be sympathetic with delusions for they are very strong. Don't try to force people to see things the way they really are because the power of Maya, Mistress of Illusion, does not intend that they shall do so until they have gone through the given experience and found out for themselves. Illusions are like mist; they cannot be fought but time dissolves them.

Every seeker after truth must learn that illusion has both good and evil effects. A child who believes in Santa Claus is happy in an illusory belief, as is the woman who falsely believes that the man she loves returns her feelings. Both, some day, will discover the truth, be hurt, and thus advance another step along the path of knowledge.

We can all be happy with our pet illusions because they can make life very pleasant until, that is, the day when we see them clearly for what they are and are forced to cope with the havoc they have created for us. Illusion is the stuff of which dreams are made, the astral sea of fancies. But the sleeper must awaken at some time and the swiftest way to do this is to search for occult knowledge.

Yet the rosy haze of illusion is created for a definite and proper purpose. It is intended – in small doses – to be a sedative for the troubled mind, permitting it to rest until the next problem arises, or to provide a temporary refuge when we are either not strong enough or not aware enough to accept the truth and tackle its consequences. At some time or another in our lives we all need to come under the spell of Maya, Mistress of Illusion, whose many-coloured veils can make life beautiful and tolerable.

Illusions lend themselves to creativity of all kinds, if only temporarily; delusions can only destroy. The dogs bay at the Moon because they are supposed to have an inbuilt sensory perception that warns them of evil and delusions were once believed to be caused by evil spirits. The crayfish, in its love life, experiences a wonderful illusion because it can fall in love with itself – until another crayfish comes along and teaches it better ways!

The self-admiring crayfish depicted on this Tarot card is like a lot of people in the world today who are so much in love with themselves that they cannot wholly love another. Such people may marry and mate, but still carry on a wonderful love affair with themselves. Other people are like the two dogs on the card, baying at the Moon. They think they are warning others of evil, demons or devils when all they are really doing is exhibiting their own inner fears under the illusory guise of giving warning, doing good, carrying out the Lord's work or whatever the cant of the day happens to be. History is full of such people, from Torqemada and his associates to the witch-burners.

Illusions can be a great solace to those who want, for whatever reason, to be wrapped firmly in the rosy tints of illusion or self-deception. So don't be too keen to disillusion others, for the power of Maya is great. She does not allow outsiders to disillusion lovers, or even self-lovers, but will awaken them herself when the time is ripe by removing her rosy veils and letting in the grey light of the illusory factor. Illusion, like the mists of the Moon, must pass away in its own time.

So the message behind card No. 18, the Moon, is that things can appear larger than life at Full Moon. Within each of us is a Moon that goes through all its phases – it is called imagination and should not be treated contemptuously. Creative imagination, the power of envisaging something and then putting that vision into action to produce a useful and concrete purpose, is all to the good. When reversed, however, this trump signifies that the individual concerned is in the grip of illusory forces, of imagination run riot, and is the erector of a pretentious facade of nonsense.

No. 19 – The Sun

The nineteenth Tarot trump, commonly called the Sun, was known to the ancients as the Lord of Success. It represents success of any kind although, on balance, it can be said to signify material achievements more than any others. Note the word achievement; it does not mean goods or riches, although these may come to the individual through the pursuit and attainment of a particular goal.

Astrologically, this card is ruled by a combination of Sun-Mercury-Jupiter forces and it should be remembered that at one time all occultism was tied to astrology; they were regarded as interconnected studies rather than as separate arts. The symbols of success are the winged wands (thoughts) of Mercury, the endurance and regularity of the Sun, and the expansive traits and rulership of Jupiter. In the Roman calendar this card was ruled by Apollo, Mercury and Jupiter; in the Greek by Phoebus, Hermes and Zeus; and in the ancient Egyptian by Amen-Ra, Thoth and Ptah, the creator.

Like happiness, success can be attained, but to expect to retain it for ever is another matter. Like the Sun, it dawns, rises to the midheaven of your life and, from that point, starts to decline until it finally sets. To expect permanent success or everlasting happiness is just childish, a hangover from fairy tale days when a fairy waved a magic wand and one's wish was granted or the prince married the princess and lived happily ever after.

Yet everybody can succeed at something, provided that they truly want to and are prepared to equip themselves properly. Firstly they will need training for the particular end in view, then application – to the exclusion of everything else. Success demands single-mindedness; it is a hard master and insists on complete devotion.

19 THE SUN

When would-be aspirants entered the Temple of Success they were told that the whole key to achievement was contained in three words; apply yourself constantly. This meant that whatever success was being sought had to be pursued continually, with all other considerations put temporarily in the background.

They were then taught that the occult powers would come to their aid if they learned how to call on them for help. To this end, they were taught to think correctly (winged wands of Mercury); to think hopefully or expansively (the sign of Jupiter, or Zeus, king of the gods) because they would become kings of their own success. Finally, they were taught to apply themselves constantly, just as the Sun is constant in its path and in its regular risings and settings. Then, with knowledge, optimism and application, they would become as the Moon in the earthy sign of Taurus, which signifies material success, or success in any required field.

But how many of us are prepared to pursue our aims so whole-heartedly? Few of us can cut ourselves off entirely from the lives and affairs of others or school our emotions so that intellect takes sole charge. The result is that we fail to achieve success in the desired aim because we allow ourselves to be constantly side-tracked.

To a great extent, we are all childlike in that anything which seems interesting can distract us from the hard work necessary to the achievement of our goals. That is why two children walking hand in hand beneath the rays of the Sun are depicted on this card. One is male, the other female, signifying that until your realise which are your positive and which your negative talents, the Sun of success cannot shine on you.

In some older packs the two figures are Castor and Pollux, the celestial twins. Each of us has a twin self – the secret, successful self we long to be. Too many of us are content to be the mundane, everyday Castor and ignore Pollux, the repressed twin who cries aloud to be released. Yet once we decide what we wish to do, develop our talents and apply them, we can take the first step towards success and happiness.

But, unless we recognise our negative traits, our individual stumbling blocks, we will encounter obstacles on the path to success and will continue to do so until we overcome our particular failings. We all tend to make the same mistakes over and over again; we all have certain weaknesses that we give in to and thus lay the seeds for future problems.

So, in order to assure future success, one must look to the past; consider past mistakes, isolate their causes and remedy these failings within ourselves. Then, and only then, can we set foot on the path to achievement. It is not a matter of just being told how to do something that ensures success, but of learning, step by step, how to make the best use of those talents that we have at our disposal.

Success in any project comes through application, hard effort, hope and determination, combined with the rewards you have earned and the wisdom you have gained in the past. No one can expect to succeed the first time they try. Often, one has to try again and again before efforts are rewarded. Success must be worked and striven for; great rewards usually only come from great efforts.

Even small achievements, those things we want to do well in, require the same dedication, the exclusion of every other interest until success is attained. To get the best out of life, it is probably better to pursue a series of small successes in a variety of things than to concentrate all your energies in achieving one overwhelming desire. A truly successful life is one that it well-balanced, with plenty of experiences: life must be lived to the full if it to have its quota of happiness and success.

Any kind of success only comes from learning, application and constancy in the pursuit of the desired aim. Luck is an entirely different matter, however; it comes unbidden and without being striven for. It can enter into anybody's life, nearly always when least expected, and will sometimes crown years of effort and determination. Most of us, though, are not born lucky and have to work hard to achieve our aims.

Failure is due to not trying hard enough or giving up too soon: it's as simple as that. Success seldom comes to those who look to others to help them along their chosen path. The idea that if you know enough important and influential people they will somehow help to make your dreams come true is a fallacy. After all, why should they help? They are your dreams, not theirs, so it is up to you to find a way to realise them yourself.

This is the arcanum behind card No. 19, the Sun. It is the trump of he who wishes to attain his objective and is prepared to make the effort necessary to do so. It is also the card of he who has succeeded in whatever he set out to do because it represents the Sun among men, the centre round which others revolve, just as the planets revolve around the Sun. It is therefore a happy augury whenever this card falls upright in a spread because it signifies the attainment of that which the enquirer most desires.

No. 20 – Judgement

Number 20 in the Major Arcana, Judgement, is usually depicted as three human figures rising from the grave and looking up towards a celestial figure blowing a trumpet, from which flies a small flag decorated with an equal-armed cross. In divination, it indicates a stage in the querent's life when an issue has reached crisis point and, once it has been resolved, changes will take place in his life.

This arcanum refers not so much to man's judgement of man or to our personal judgement of a given situation, but to an assessment of our own stage of development that necessitates a change in order that we may develop further. Thus it represents divine judgement on the actions of the individual and forecasts the effects that must succeed the cause.

Some of us are not in the least capable of judging ourselves – our own capabilities, character and talent. And there are millions of people in unhappy circumstances who long for their lot to be improved but simply will not make the effort to improve it by their own endeavour because they are afraid they will fail. Such people do not wait for divine judgement but weigh themselves in the balance, thereby condemning themselves in advance as failures or incompetents.

Yet divine judgement should not be feared since it can bring great rewards and happiness besides punishment. So card No. 20 can be a card of promise as well as one of warning. The initial effort must come from the individual, then divine judgement can play its proper part; but pre-judge yourself, having made no such effort, and you may be found guilty. You will then have condemned yourself instead of allowing events and destiny to be your judge.

It is foolish and unnecessary to be your own executioner for the world itself is often only too anxious to condemn you. So do not burden yourself with this unsavoury task; instead, give yourself a little encouragement if you have no friends to bolster your ego and make a conscious effort towards achieving your ends. Decide what it is that you really need and then strive for it with energy and purpose. But always remember that you will reap what you sow; therefore your intentions, too, must be right.

It is no good doing someone a service if your action is based on ill-intent, nor is it going to weigh in your favour if you achieve your material objectives through selfish motives. The creative power that made the universe also made you; the power is the true judge, rewarder or punisher and can mete out reward or punishment for intentions as well as actions and achievements. And this divine weighing in the balance takes place not only at the last judgement – death – but at other points in earthly life, too.

Such occasions are symbolised by card No. 20 and there are times in all our lives when we come under judgement followed by major changes. It is as though we were in a train running on a certain track when suddenly the points are changed and the train is derailed or re-routed onto another track. The new route may be a far easier one or it can be a very bumpy ride; this will depend on the outcome of the judgement passed on us for our past actions.

In every experience in life we must exercise judgement. When we decide for ourselves that this or that is right, that we will or will not do a certain thing, we often gloss over our true motives. These are often

122

selfish, but we convince ourselves that we are acting from the highest possible motives. Yet the law of judgement still operates and whether the course we decide to take turns out well or otherwise depends solely on our reasons for taking it.

Most of us have probably experienced a stroke of what seemed like gross injustice at some time in our lives and racked our brains to find out just why whatever it was should have happened to us. Also, we cannot have helped wondering why some people suffer crippling handicaps and misfortunes while others enjoy all the good things that life has to offer. When there is no apparent explanation, we must assume that there is a karmic reason for such situations: it is the price being paid for something done in the past, in a former incarnation.

If we have but one life to live, what decides the unbalance, the seeming unfairness? This is the argument for reincarnation; and if we do not accept reincarnation but regard this earthly life as the only one we have to live, then we will never understand the mysteries of trump No. 20. For this card shows that we have reached a critical point in our lives and affairs: one that is not confined to our present life but is related to our past karmas, to what we have earned – good or bad – from our former incarnations.

Perhaps the simplest way to explain this is to say that in past lives we had as many human failings and as many virtues as we possess now; sometimes we lived out the worst side of our natures, sometimes the best. Whatever we have done in our past lives has been recorded and, in our present existence, we reap the rewards – good or bad – for these past actions, for there always comes a time of reckoning.

This card signifies such times of reckoning and, even if the judgement goes against us, once we have paid the penalty in full we reach the stage where unsuspected blessings can come our way. But human nature is very odd: although we can usually accept that we had to be punished, we can't so easily accept that afterwards we shall be blessed. Yet this is indeed so; once we have been tried, condemned, punished, pardoned and released from our debts, that which was good in our karma is then able to come our way.

If you don't believe this, think back to the trials and periods of unhappiness in your life. After a time, did not some compensatory factor become apparent? Can you honestly say that you have never been in the position where you have said to yourself, 'That had to happen, otherwise this could not have been done?'

Those who have just passed the stage represented by Judgement will probably be wondering how long their lives are going to remain in chaos and how long it will be before compensatory factors enter their lives again. Well, it depends on the size of the debt to be paid, of course, but there has to be a turning point some time. Usually the third anniversary of your particular crisis marks the turning point in your affairs, although advancement on the occult path and in occult knowledge stirs up karmic forces rather more quickly than if your are occultly unaware.

But with knowledge comes the strength to cope and understand and thus survive life's trials. So don't worry about what may happen; most probably it won't – the worst of our worries are those which never happen! And, even if trouble does come your way, you will be able to cope because divine judgement is just and, unlike that of man, is tempered with mercy.

No. 21 – The World

Number 21 of the Major Arcana is called the World and in any divinatory spread signifies the personal world of the enquirer. Wherever this card falls in a spread, it is a hopeful omen, with special emphasis in certain placements. Even if reversed, the omen is still good for the achievement of the enquirer's personal ambitions in the future although these will be delayed for the present. It is, then, a hopeful and uplifting card because it is linked with the Wheel of Fortune turning in the querent's favour.

The world of success differs for every person, but Tarot card No. 21 signifies that the private world of the enquirer – his personal hopes and ambitions – will be fulfilled and success will reward his efforts. We all create our own worlds for ourselves and trump No. 21 represents the powers awaiting development that lie within each of us.

The arcanum of this card is connected with the Four Pillars of Earth which are depicted symbolically as the bull, lion, eagle and man in the four corners of this card. These, in turn, represent the four seasons and coincide with the zodiacal signs Taurus (spring), Leo (summer), Scorpio (autumn) and Aquarius (winter); they also correspond to the four elements of Earth, Fire, Water and Air respectively.

These are the seasons of life and the pictorial symbolism on this card points out the strengths and weaknesses of the various seasons. This is obviously a very ancient arcanum because it derives from an age when Taurus was the first sign of the zodiac. Now, of course, Aries holds this position but this was not always so and Taurus was once the sign that started the zodiacal year. The Tarot is very ancient and some of its original symbolism has been retained, which explains why the Pillars of Earth, representing the seasons, seem to be a sign behind those in modern usage.

The bull represents youth and the springtime of life, with all its physical strength, its wild enthusiasms, recklessness and intolerance.

The lion signifies adulthood or maturity, when each person has had time to develop his inner powers and can tackle life with dignity and tolerance. The unthinking enthusiasms of youth are now past and experience has – or should have – tempered and developed the individual.

The eagle's time is the autumn of life, middle age and after, when all the powers of the developed mind and treasures of experience cooperate with shrewdness and insight. It is a time when the individual accepts things as they are rather than as it was once hoped they would be; it is the season of calm fruitfulness. Lastly comes the symbol of man, signifying winter or old age. Each season in life has its difficulties and its triumphs; each brings its sorrows and rewards; yet we are all masters of ourselves and thus create our own worlds.

Every man and woman has a secret world, a world in which they see themselves achieving success and happiness. Some want public acclaim and the fruits of fame; others want only personal happiness and security. Each strives after his particular goal in his own way, often handicapped by not understanding the latent powers and talents that lie within. Between what a person is and what he wants to be is a great gulf that, at times, seems unbridgeable. Yet this is not really the case because, if one finds and uses correctly those talents with which one is born, they form the foundation stones on which success and happiness can be built.

Each of us has some talent which, if applied vigorously, can bring success in its train. True, there will be many ups and downs, but success is bound to follow in the end. Just to daydream of success is to dissipate it; to attempt it, though, is to develop success. Talent deserves a chance to prove itself and your particular talent usually lies in the sphere that most attracts you. If one particular thing holds appeal, it usually denotes that there is a talent for that specific subject; it is the suppressed talent inside the individual that makes the appeal, calling out to be used.

In order to achieve success and happiness, each of us must discover his own talents and apply them; it is no good burying them in the sands of wishful thinking. Failure in our goals is the result of not trying to gain our heart's desire or else of setting about it in the wrong way. Wishing for success, unbacked by effort, is of no avail. But striving towards success means that we are employing immense forces that thrust like a spear through all obstacles between us and our objectives.

No effort to achieve success is ever wasted. The mental and physical power behind each attempt accumulates on the astral plane; it is placed in our 'occult bank' until the time comes when we have enough power to our credit to overthrow every barrier to our success and our private worlds of happiness can be achieved. So, card No.21 is a fortunate omen in any divinatory spread because it usually denotes that applied effort is about to meet with success in proportion to the effort expended. This last point should be noted: we cannot get out of life more than we put in.

We are all, to some extent, the victims of our own self-indulgence because we tend to look for the easy way of getting through life and may, therefore, neglect inborn abilities. Some, indeed, are afraid of success itself because of the responsibilities it can bring; others fail because they do not understand themselves, they have not learned life's lessons. Life itself is the great initiator, its trials and tribulations are there for us to learn from and, if we learn our lessons correctly, we will receive our just rewards, we will attain the laurel wreath depicted on card No. 21, the World.

When we have learned from our errors, when we have learned wisdom through our experiences and resisted or overcome the temptations of the Devil, when we have survived the destruction wrought by the Tower Struck by Lightning and rebuilt our lives by utilising our hidden talents and developing our mental and spiritual resources, then – and only then – are we ready for the rewards implicit in the card called the World.

At some time or another in our lives, we do attain our own little worlds and our individual cups of happiness are filled – perhaps for a short time, maybe for longer. At such times we should realise that others have not attained theirs, or perhaps have overturned their cups and lost the happiness they contained. So, while we are enjoying the fruits of our own labours – our own happiness – we must spare time and effort to help others who are not so fortunate. If we don't, if we hold on to what we think is ours for selfish reasons, then we are in danger of upsetting our own cup of happiness; our own little world can be turned upside down, and we may lose all that we have gained.

Yet, if we have truly learned life's lessons, if we have achieved a perfect state of balance in our own natures, if we have completed our initiatory journey through life, then the rewards are great and enduring because we have then obtained control over the material world which is, itself, the lowest aspect of the spiritual.

Index